The Letters of the Korean Alphabet

The Korean language is the official language of both North Korea and South Korea. The Korean language is written using the Korean alphabet letters called Hangul (also spelled Hangeul).

Hangul was invented by King Sejong the Great in the 15th century. Hangul includes consonant and vowel letters composed of straight or curved lines and circles. King Sejong the Great created the consonant letters inspired by the shape of speech organs when each consonant sound is produced. The vowel letters were created using the symbols which represent the three elements of nature: sky, humans, and the earth.

Modern Hangul consists of 40 letters including 19 consonants and 21 vowels. Each letter has its sound value and all sounds in the Korean language are made by combining the letters of consonants and vowels. Korean words are written using a syllable block from left to right and from top to bottom. The syllable block always begins with the initial consonant(s), then the vowel(s) are arranged vertically or horizontally, and one or two more consonants could follow to the bottom.

TRACK 1 — Consonants

Basic	ㄱ g	ㄴ n	ㄷ d	ㄹ r or l	ㅁ m	ㅂ b	ㅅ s	ㅇ silent or ng	ㅈ j
Double	ㄲ kk		ㄸ tt			ㅃ pp	ㅆ ss		ㅉ jj
Heavy	ㅋ k		ㅌ t			ㅍ p		ㅎ h	ㅊ ch

TRACK 2 — Vowels

Single	ㅏ a		ㅓ eo		ㅣ i	ㅗ o	ㅜ u	ㅡ eu	
Double	ㅑ ya	ㅐ ae	ㅒ yae	ㅕ yeo	ㅖ e	ㅖ ye	ㅛ yo	ㅠ yu	
	ㅘ wa	ㅙ wae	ㅚ oe	ㅝ weo	ㅞ we	ㅟ wi	ㅢ ui		

Chart Showing Consonant + Vowel Combinations

This chart shows the most commonly used consonants and vowels of the Hangul alphabet, and how they are combined to make syllables. The consonants are on the left axis of the chart and the vowels are along the top. The combinations are shown in the table.

Vowels / Consonants	ㅏ a	ㅑ ya	ㅓ eo	ㅕ yeo	ㅗ o	ㅛ yo	ㅜ u	ㅠ yu	ㅡ eu	ㅣ i
ㄱ g	가 ga	갸 gya	거 geo	겨 gyeo	고 go	교 gyo	구 gu	규 gyu	그 geu	기 gi
ㄴ n	나 na	냐 nya	너 neo	녀 nyeo	노 no	뇨 nyo	누 nu	뉴 nyu	느 neu	니 ni
ㄷ d	다 da	댜 dya	더 deo	뎌 dyeo	도 do	됴 dyo	두 du	듀 dyu	드 deu	디 di
ㄹ l (r)	라 la	랴 lya	러 leo	려 lyeo	로 lo	료 lyo	루 lu	류 lyu	르 leu	리 li
ㅁ m	마 ma	먀 mya	머 meo	며 myeo	모 mo	묘 myo	무 mu	뮤 myu	므 meu	미 mi
ㅂ b	바 ba	뱌 bya	버 beo	벼 byeo	보 bo	뵤 byo	부 bu	뷰 byu	브 beu	비 bi
ㅅ s	사 sa	샤 sya	서 seo	셔 syeo	소 so	쇼 syo	수 su	슈 syu	스 seu	시 si
ㅇ silent / ng	아 a	야 ya	어 eo	여 yeo	오 o	요 yo	우 u	유 yu	으 eu	이 i
ㅈ j	자 ja	쟈 jya	저 jeo	져 jyeo	조 jo	죠 jyo	주 ju	쥬 jyu	즈 jeu	지 ji
ㅊ ch	차 cha	챠 chya	처 cheo	쳐 chyeo	초 cho	쵸 chyo	추 chu	츄 chyu	츠 cheu	치 chi
ㅋ k	카 ka	캬 kya	커 keo	켜 kyeo	코 ko	쿄 kyo	쿠 ku	큐 kyu	크 keu	키 ki
ㅌ t	타 ta	탸 tya	터 teo	텨 tyeo	토 to	툐 tyo	투 tu	튜 tyu	트 teu	티 ti
ㅍ p	파 pa	퍄 pya	퍼 peo	펴 pyeo	포 po	표 pyo	푸 pu	퓨 pyu	프 peu	피 pi
ㅎ h	하 ha	햐 hya	허 heo	혀 hyeo	호 ho	효 hyo	후 hu	휴 hyu	흐 heu	히 hi
ㄲ kk	까 kka	꺄 kkya	꺼 kkeo	껴 kkyeo	꼬 kko	꾜 kkyo	꾸 kku	뀨 kkyu	끄 kkeu	끼 kki
ㄸ tt	따 tta	땨 ttya	떠 tteo	뗘 ttyeo	또 tto	뚀 ttyo	뚜 ttu	뜌 ttyu	뜨 tteu	띠 tti
ㅃ pp	빠 ppa	뺘 ppya	뻐 ppeo	뼈 ppyeo	뽀 ppo	뾰 ppyo	뿌 ppu	쀼 ppyu	쁘 ppeu	삐 ppi
ㅆ ss	싸 ssa	쌰 ssya	써 sseo	쎠 ssyeo	쏘 sso	쑈 ssyo	쑤 ssu	쓔 ssyu	쓰 sseu	씨 ssi
ㅉ jj	짜 jja	쨔 jjya	쩌 jjeo	쪄 jjyeo	쪼 jjo	쬬 jjyo	쭈 jju	쮸 jjyu	쯔 jjeu	찌 jji

Practice Writing Hangul Letters

Forming the letters of Korean alphabet is easy! There are just two basic rules: horizontal strokes are written from left to right and vertical strokes are written from top to bottom, just as in English.

Let's write the consonants:

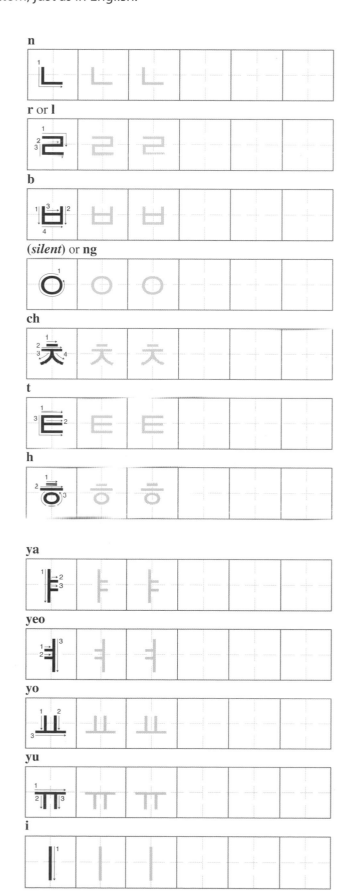

g

n

d

r or l

m

b

s

(*silent*) or ng

j

ch

k

t

p

h

Now, let's write the vowels:

a

ya

eo

yeo

o

yo

u

yu

eu

i

On the following pages you will learn to write the main syllable combinations that are used in Hangul.

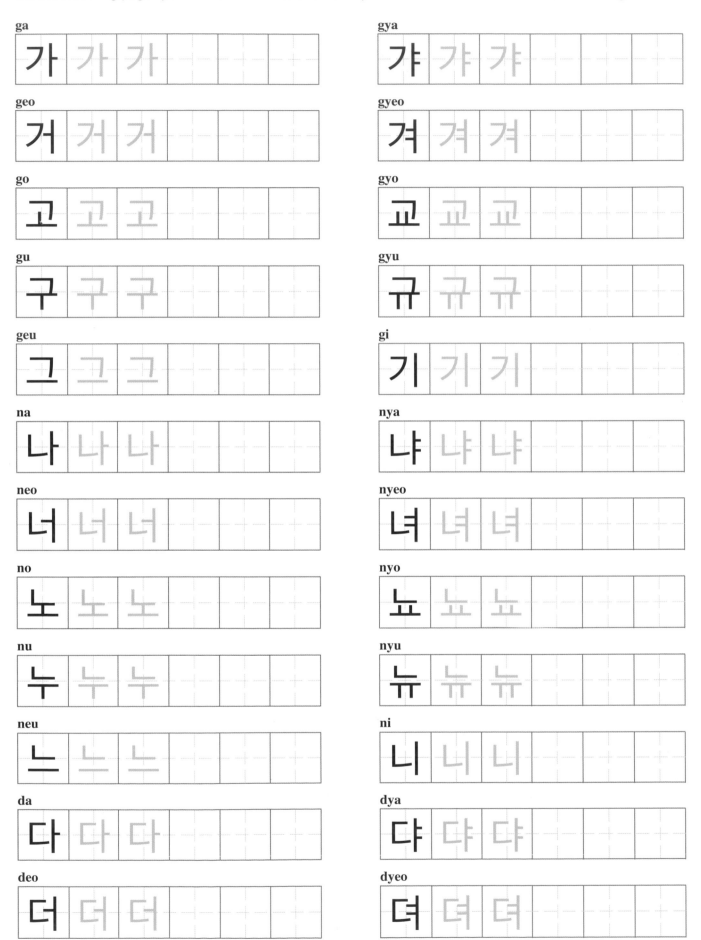

ga 가

gya 갸

geo 거

gyeo 겨

go 고

gyo 교

gu 구

gyu 규

geu 그

gi 기

na 나

nya 냐

neo 너

nyeo 녀

no 노

nyo 뇨

nu 누

nyu 뉴

neu 느

ni 니

da 다

dya 댜

deo 더

dyeo 뎌

do

du

deu

la

leo

lo

lu

leu

ma

meo

mo

mu

dyo

dyu

di

lya

lyeo

lyo

lyu

li

mya

myeo

myo

myu

5

meu
므 므 므

mi
미 미 미

ba
바 바 바

bya
뱌 뱌 뱌

beo
버 버 버

byeo
벼 벼 벼

bo
보 보 보

byo
뵤 뵤 뵤

bu
부 부 부

byu
뷰 뷰 뷰

beu
브 브 브

bi
비 비 비

sa
사 사 사

sya
샤 샤 샤

seo
서 서 서

syeo
셔 셔 셔

so
소 소 소

syo
쇼 쇼 쇼

su
수 수 수

syu
슈 슈 슈

seu
스 스 스

si
시 시 시

a
아 아 아

ya
야 야 야

chu
추 추 추

chyu
츄 츄 츄

cheu
츠 츠 츠

chi
치 치 치

ka
카 카 카

kya
캬 캬 캬

keo
커 커 커

kyeo
켜 켜 켜

ko
코 코 코

kyo
쿄 쿄 쿄

ku
쿠 쿠 쿠

kyu
큐 큐 큐

keu
크 크 크

ki
키 키 키

ta
타 타 타

tya
탸 탸 탸

teo
터 터 터

tyeo
텨 텨 텨

to
토 토 토

tyo
툐 툐 툐

tu
투 투 투

tyu
튜 튜 튜

teu
트 트 트

ti
티 티 티

pa 파

pya 퍄

peo 퍼

pyeo 펴

po 포

pyo 표

pu 푸

pyu 퓨

peu 프

pi 피

ha 하

hya 햐

heo 허

hyeo 혀

ho 호

hyo 효

hu 후

hyu 휴

heu 흐

hi 히

kka 까

kkya 꺄

kkeo 꺼

kkyeo 껴

kko

꼬 꼬 꼬

kkyo

꾜 꾜 꾜

kku

꾸 꾸 꾸

kkyu

뀨 뀨 뀨

kkeu

끄 끄 끄

kki

끼 끼 끼

tta

따 따 따

ttya

땨 땨 땨

tteo

떠 떠 떠

ttyeo

뗘 뗘 뗘

tto

또 또 또

ttyo

뚀 뚀 뚀

ttu

뚜 뚜 뚜

ttyu

뜌 뜌 뜌

tteu

뜨 뜨 뜨

tti

띠 띠 띠

ppa

빠 빠 빠

ppya

뺘 뺘 뺘

ppeo

뻐 뻐 뻐

ppyeo

뼈 뼈 뼈

ppo

뽀 뽀 뽀

ppyo

뾰 뾰 뾰

ppu

뿌 뿌 뿌

ppyu

쀼 쀼 쀼

ppeu 뿌

ppi 삐

ssa 싸

ssya 쌰

sseo 써

ssyeo 쎠

sso 쏘

ssyo 쑈

ssu 쑤

ssyu 쓔

sseu 쓰

ssi 씨

jia 짜

jjya 쨔

jjeo 쩌

jjyeo 쪄

jjo 쪼

jjyo 쬬

jju 쭈

jjyu 쮸

jjeu 쯔

jji 찌

11

Daily Expressions

안녕하세요? **annyeonghaseyo** Hello.

안녕하세요

어떻게 지내세요? **eotteoke jinaeseyo** How are you?

어떻게 지내세요

어서 오세요. **eoseooseyo** Welcome

어서 오세요

잘 지내요. **jal jinaeyo** I am fine.

잘 지내요

오랜만이에요. **oraenmanieyo** It's been a long time.

오랜만이에요

반가워요. **bangawoyo** Nice to meet you.

반가워요

안녕히 가세요. **annyeonghi gaseyo** Good-bye. (to person leaving when you are staying)

안녕히 가세요

안녕히 계세요. **annyeonghi gyeseyo** Good-bye. (to person staying when you are leaving)

안녕히 계세요

나중에 봐요. **najunge bwayo** See you later.

나중에 봐요

잘 자요. **jal jayo** Good night.

잘 자요

네. **ne** Yes.

네

아니요. **aniyo** No.

아니요

고마워요. **gomawoyo** Thank you.

고마워요

천만에요. **cheonmaneyo** You are welcome.

천만에요

미안해요. **mianhaeyo** I am sorry.

미안해요

실례합니다. **sillyehamnida** Excuse me.

실례합니다

잠시만요. **jamsimanyo** Wait a moment.

잠시만요

화이팅! **hwaiting** Good luck! (Lit. fighting)

화이팅

축하해요. **chukahaeyo** Congratulations

축하해요

진짜요? **jinjjayo** Is it true?

진짜요

얼마예요? **eolmayeyo** How much is it?

얼마예요

여보세요. **yeoboseyo** Hello. (on the phone)

여보세요

Korean Food

밥 **bap** cooked rice

밥

떡 **tteok** rice cake

떡

반찬 **banchan** side dish

반 찬

김치 **gimchi** kimchi

김 치

김밥 **kimbap** seaweed rice roll

김 밥

갈비 **galbi** grilled ribs

갈 비

라면 **ramyeon** ramen

라 면

찌개 **jjigae** stew

찌 개

치맥 **chimaek** fried chicken and beer

치 맥

비빔밥 **bibimbap** bibimbap

비 빔 밥

불고기 **bulgogi** bulgogi

불 고 기

떡볶이 **tteokbokki** stir-fried rice cake

떡 볶 이

삼겹살 **samgyeopsal** grilled pork belly

삼 겹 살

삼계탕 **samgyetang** chicken soup with ginseng

삼 계 탕

식혜 **sikye** sweet rice punch

식 혜

소주 **soju** soju

소 주

막걸리 **makgeolli** Korean rice wine

막 걸 리

먹방 **meokbang** mukbang (eating show)

먹 방

건배! **geonbae** Cheers!

건 배

소주를 마셔요. **sojureul masyeoyo** (I) drink soju.

소 주 를 마 셔 요

매워요. **maewoyo** It is spicy.

매 워 요

맛있어요. **masisseoyo** It is tasty.

맛 있 어 요

맛있게 드세요. **masitge deuseyo** Enjoy your meal.

맛 있 게 드 세 요

K-Pop and K-Drama

케이팝 **keipap** K-Pop

케	이	팝							

케이드라마 **keideurama** K-Drama

케	이	드	라	마					

한류 **hallyu** Korean Wave

한	류								

가수 **gasu** singer

가	수								

배우 **baeu** actor

배	우								

꽃미남 **kkonminam** handsome man

꽃	미	남							

아이돌 그룹 **aidol geurup** idol groups

아	이	돌	그	룹					

팬 **paen** fan (a person)

팬									

올킬 **olkil** number 1 on all charts (Lit. All-Kill)

올	킬								

가사 **gasa** lyrics

가	사								

컴백 **keombaek** coming back with new music

컴	백								

주인공   **juingong**   main character

주 인 공

막장   **makjang**   plots involving ridiculous situations

막 장

반전이 있어요.   **banjeoni isseoyo**   It has a plot twist.

반 전 이 있 어 요

노래를 잘해요.   **noraereul jalhaeyo**   (A person) sings well.

노 래 를 잘 해 요

춤을 잘 춰요.   **chumeul jal chwoyo**   (A person) dances well.

춤 을 잘 춰 요

연기를 잘해요.   **yeongireul jalhaeyo**   (A person) acts well.

연 기 를 잘 해 요

짱   **jjang**   Awesome!

짱

대박!   **daebak**   Amazing! (Lit. jackpot)

대 박

케이팝을 들어요.   **keipabeul deureoyo**   (I) listen to K-Pop.

케 이 팝 을 들 어 요

케이팝을 좋아해요   **keipabeul joahaeyo**   (I) like K-Pop.

케 이 팝 을 좋 아 해 요

사랑해요.   **saranghaeyo**   I love you.

사 랑 해 요

Social Media

인스타그램 **inseutageuraem** Instagram

인스타그램

트위터 **teuwiteo** Twitter

트위터

페이스북 **peiseubuk** Facebook

페이스북

유튜브 **yutyubeu** YouTube

유튜브

브이앱 **beuiaep** V Live

브이앱

에스엔에스 **eseueneseu** social networking service (SNS)

에스엔에스

블로그 **beullogeu** blog

블로그

동영상 **dongyeongsang** video

동영상

인싸 **inssa** a person who has many friends (Lit. insider)

인싸

아싸 **assa** a person who doesn't have many friends (Lit. outsider)

아싸

팔로워 **pallowo** follower

팔로워

인플루언서 **inpeullueonseo** influencer

인플루언서

프로필 **peuropil** profile

프로필

구독 **gudok** subscription

구독

악플 **akpeul** malicious comment

악플

삭제 **sakje** deletion

삭제

검색 **geomsaek** search

검색

친구 추가 **chingu chuga** adding someone as a friend

친구추가

댓글을 달아요. **daetgeureul darayo** (I) write a comment.

댓글을달아요

사진을 올려요. **sajineul ollyeoyo** (I) upload a photo.

사진을올려요

팔로우해요. **pallouhaeyo** (I) follow.

팔로우해요

언팔해요. **eonpalhaeyo** (I) unfollow.

언팔해요

'좋아요'를 눌러요. **joayoreul nulleoyo** (I) tap the LIKE button.

좋아요를눌러요

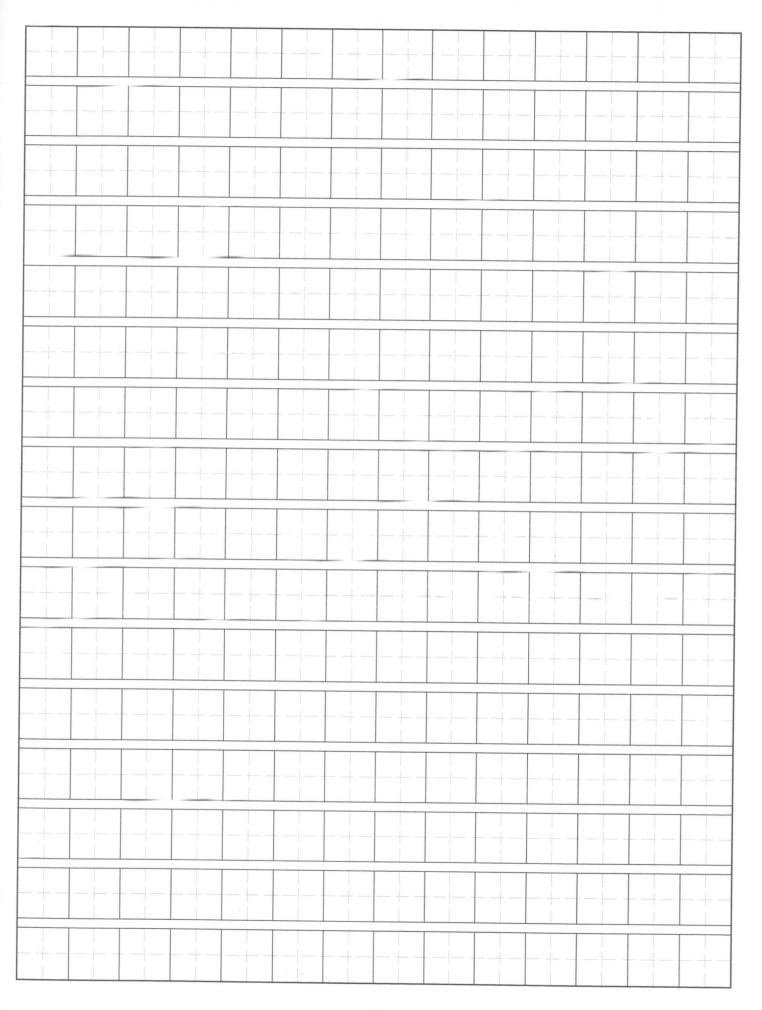

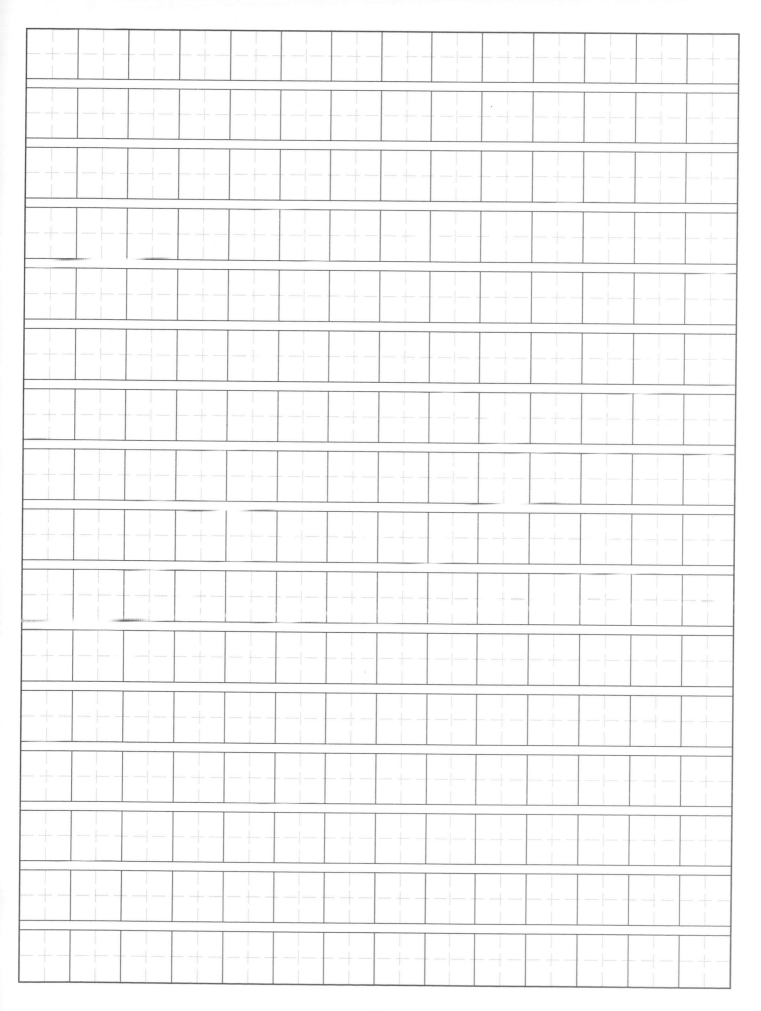

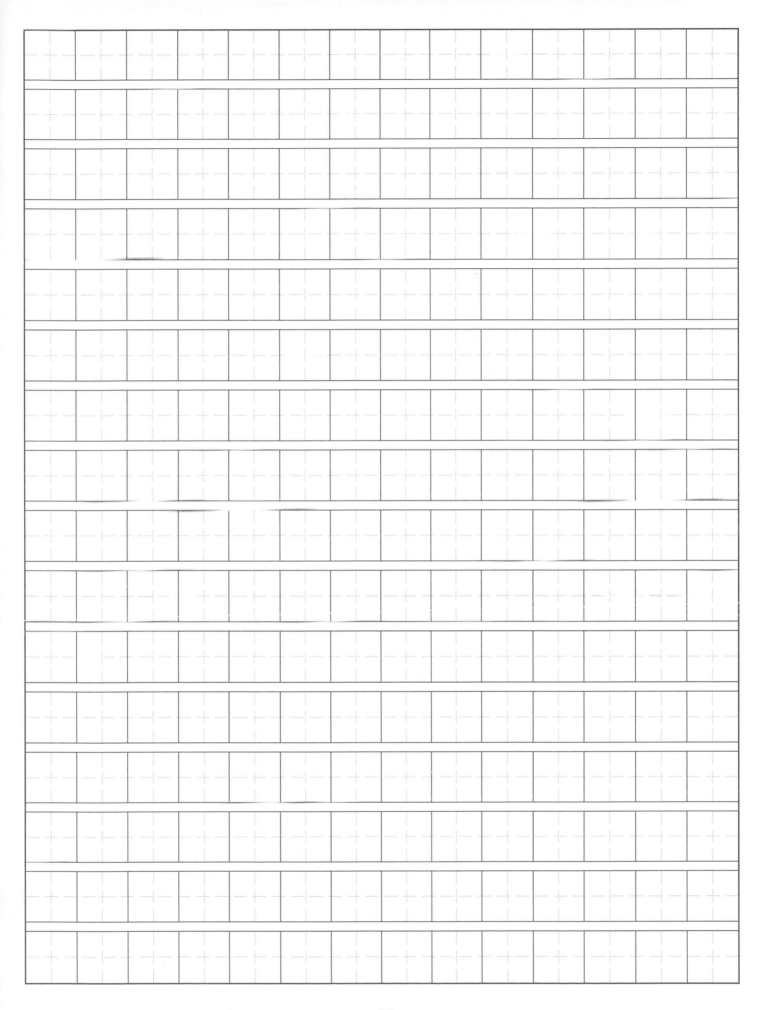

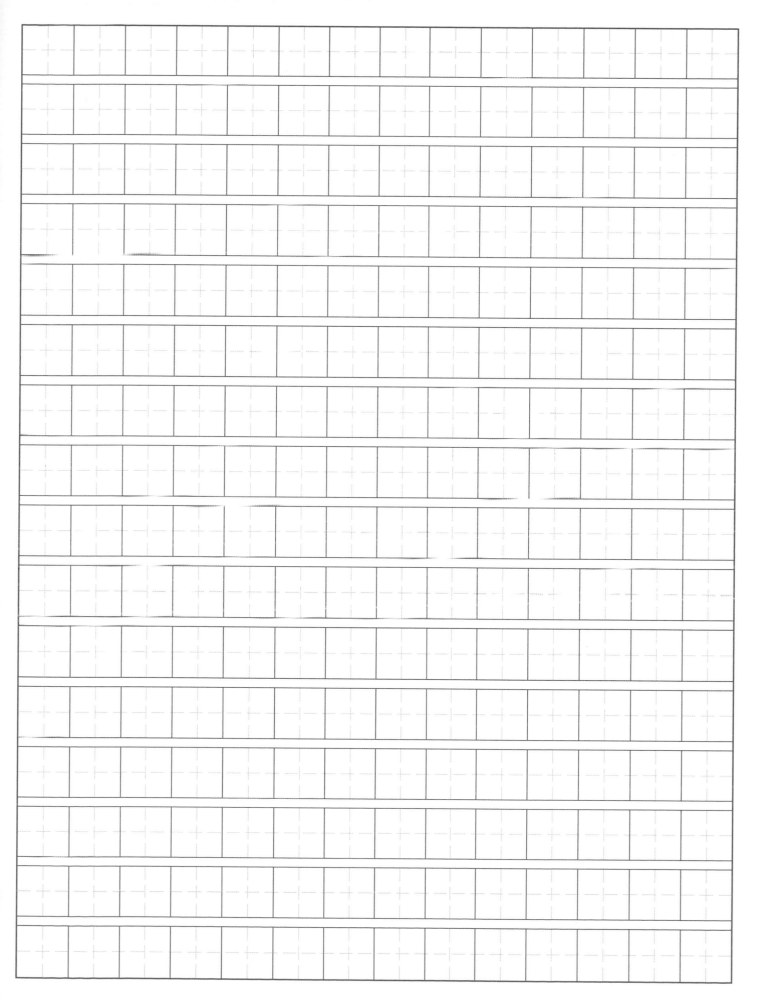

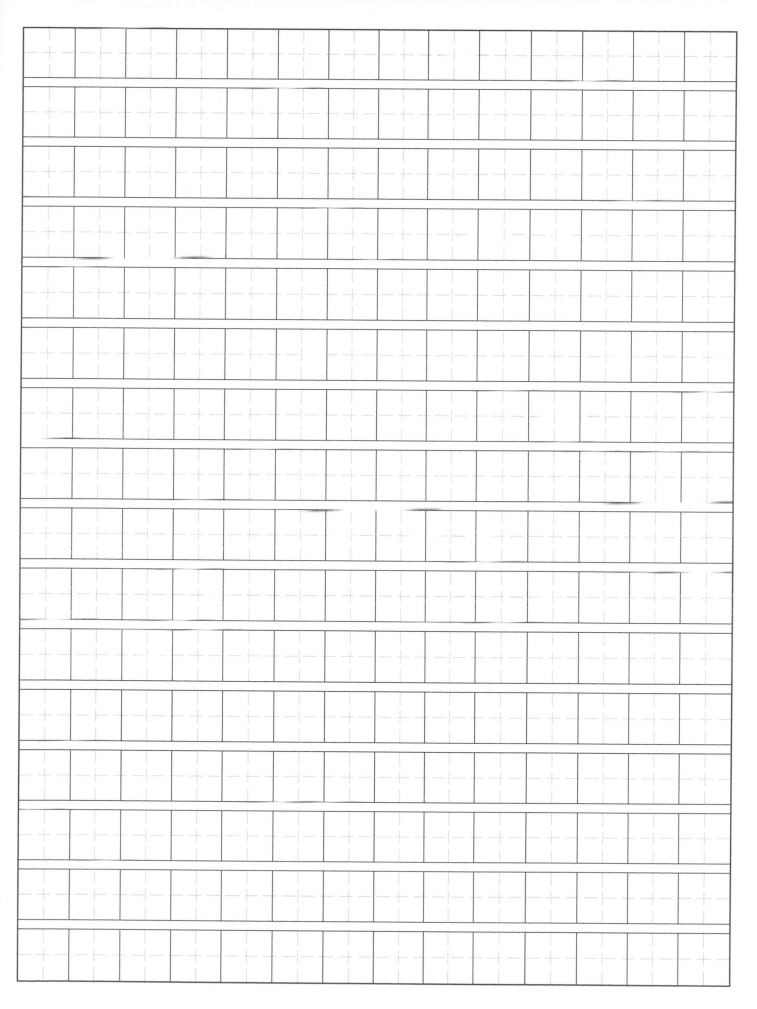

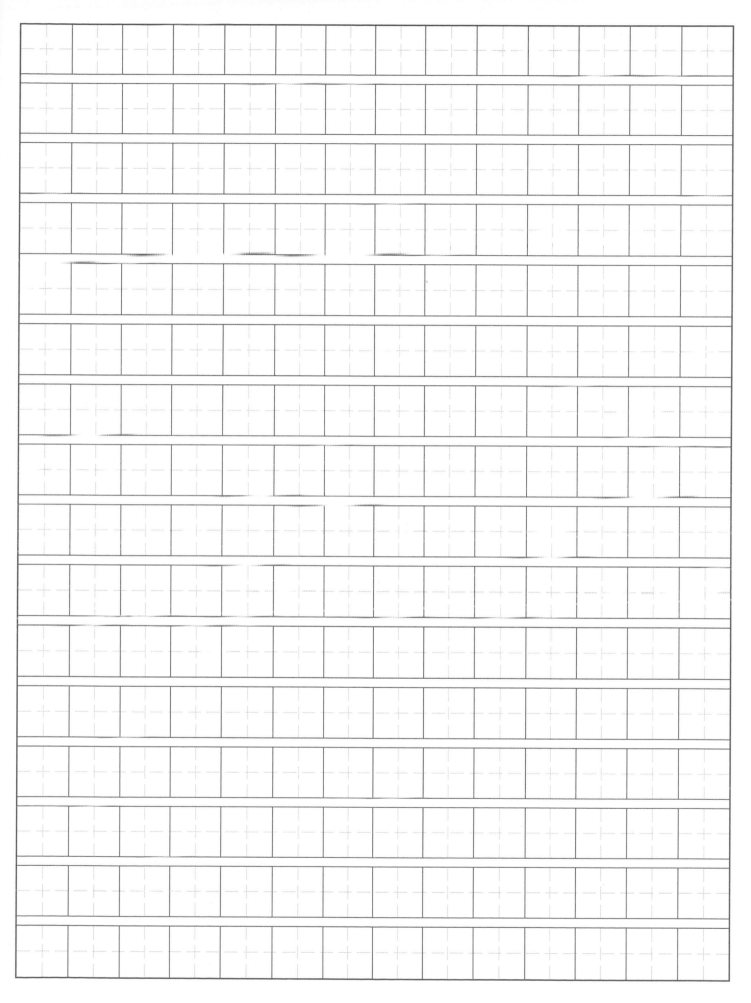

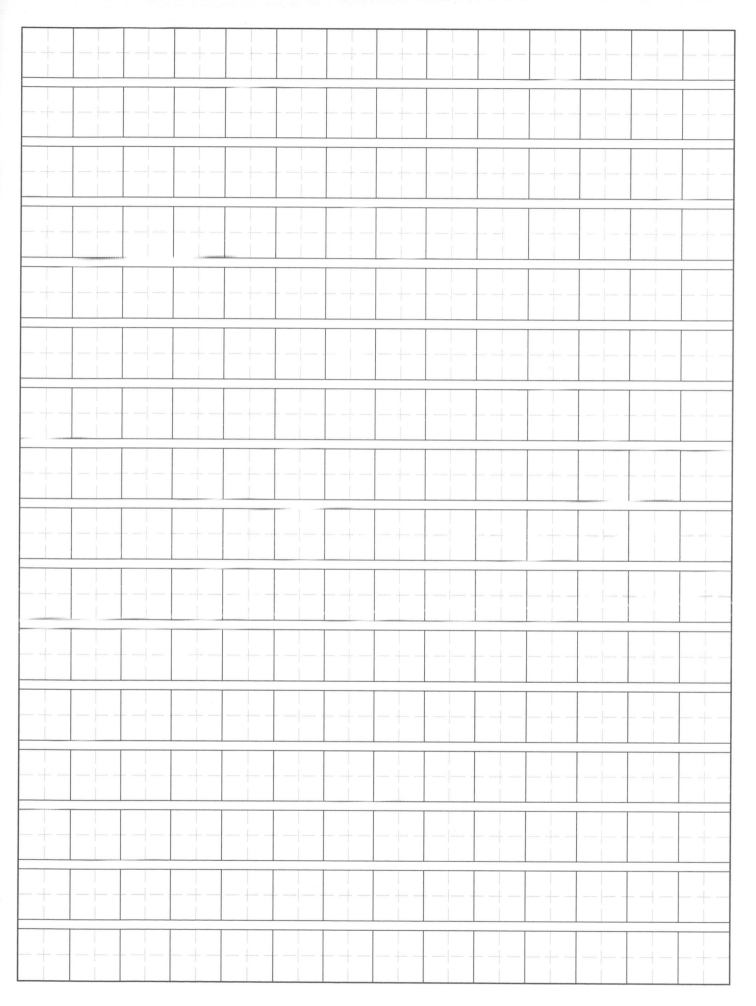

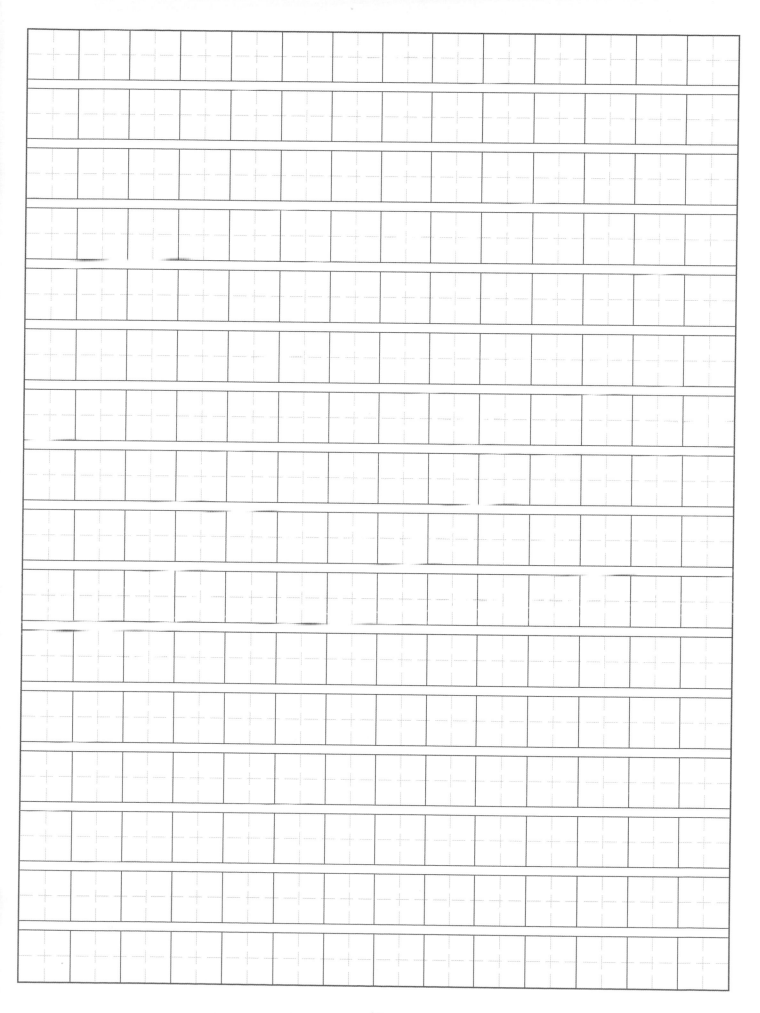

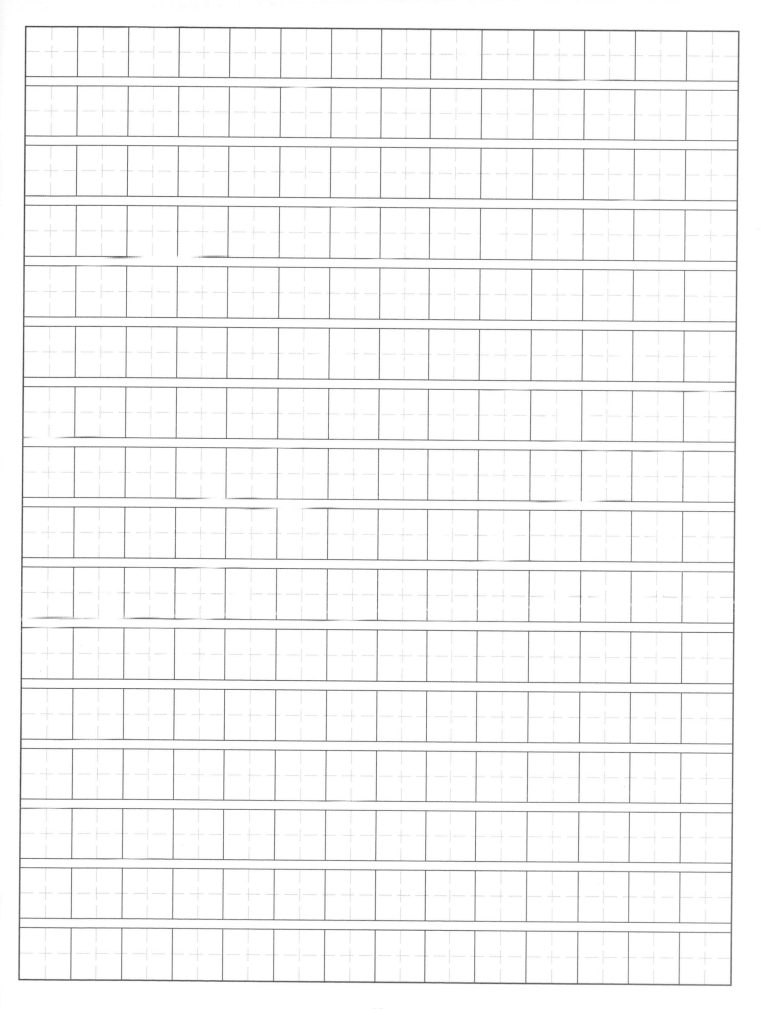

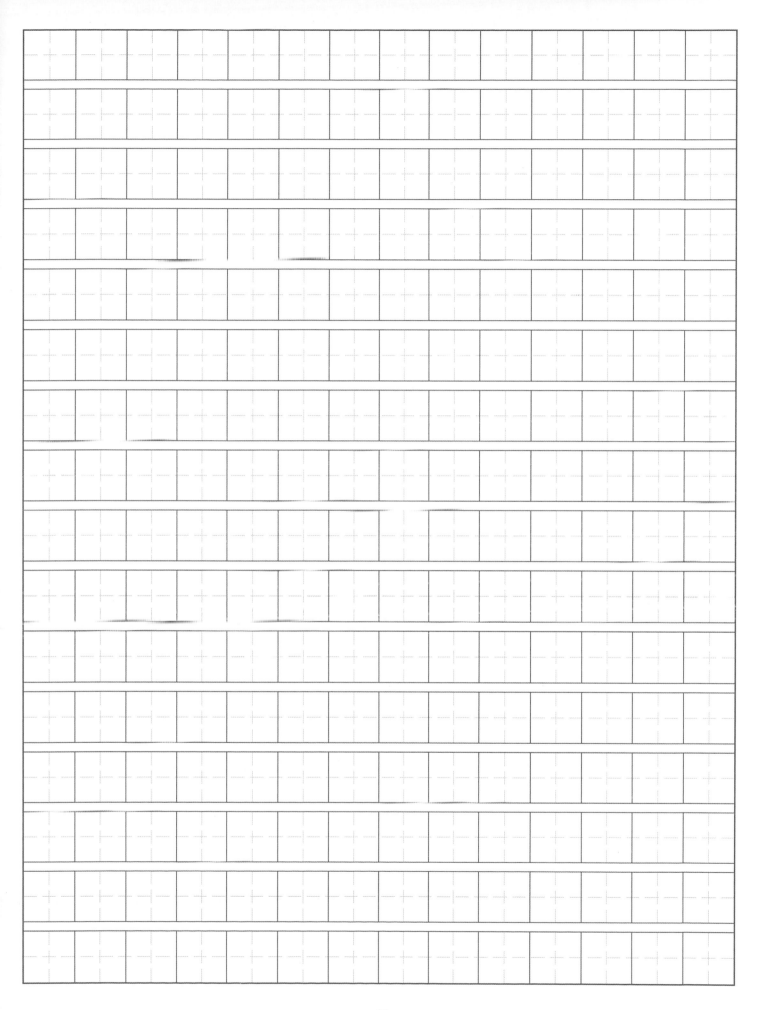

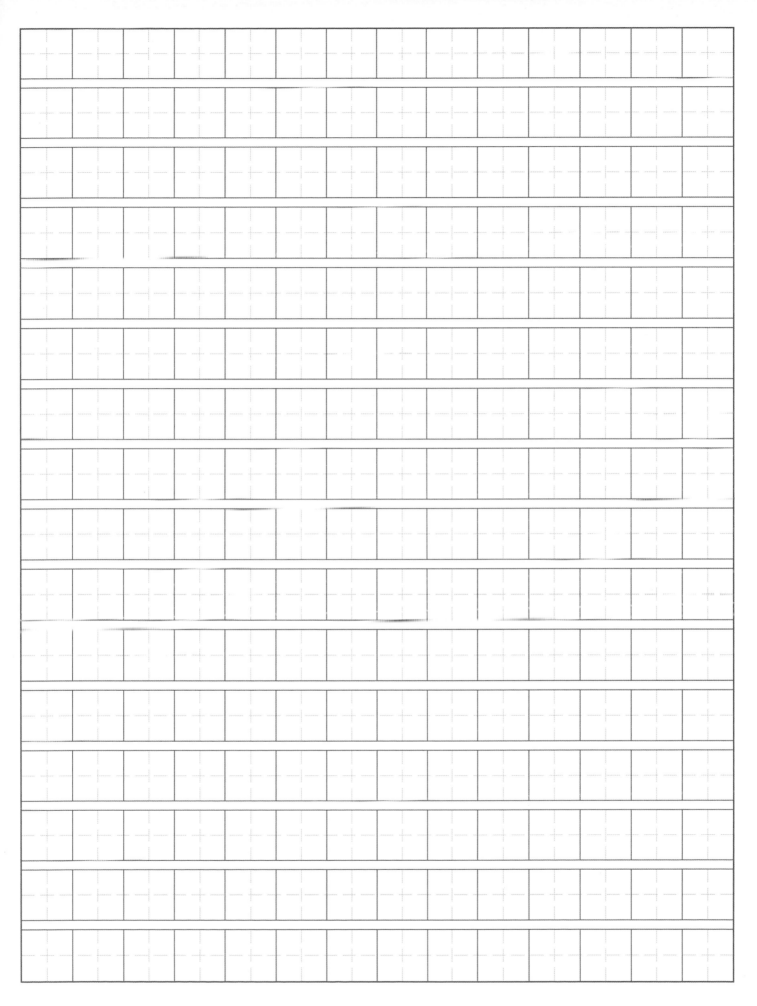

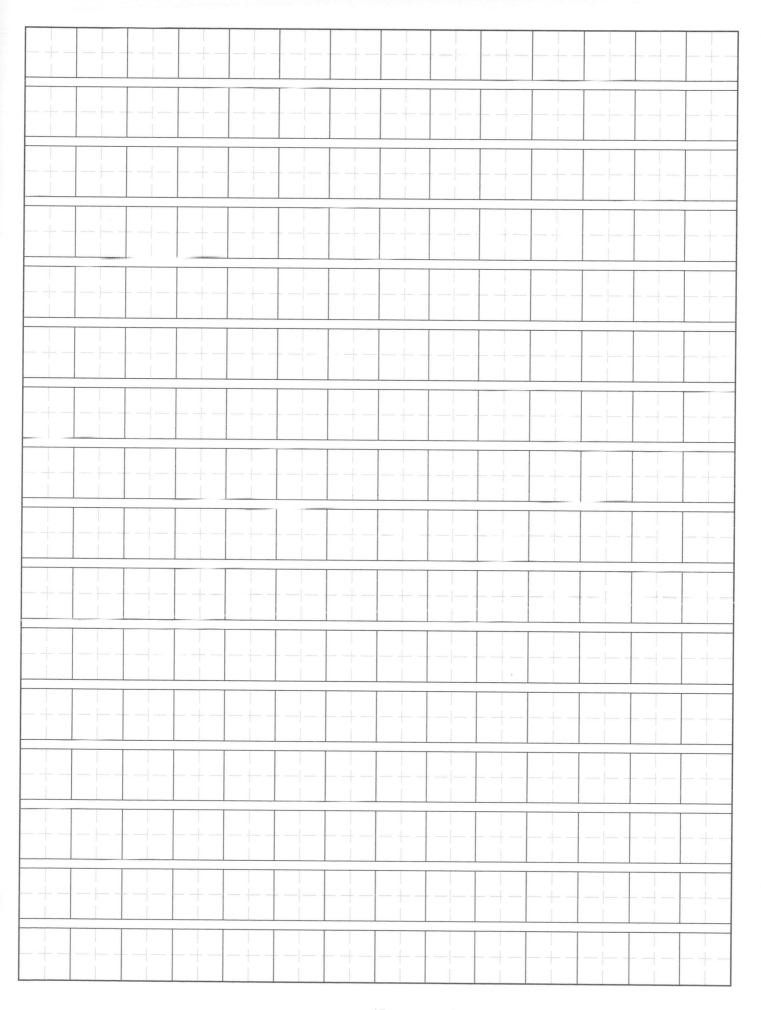

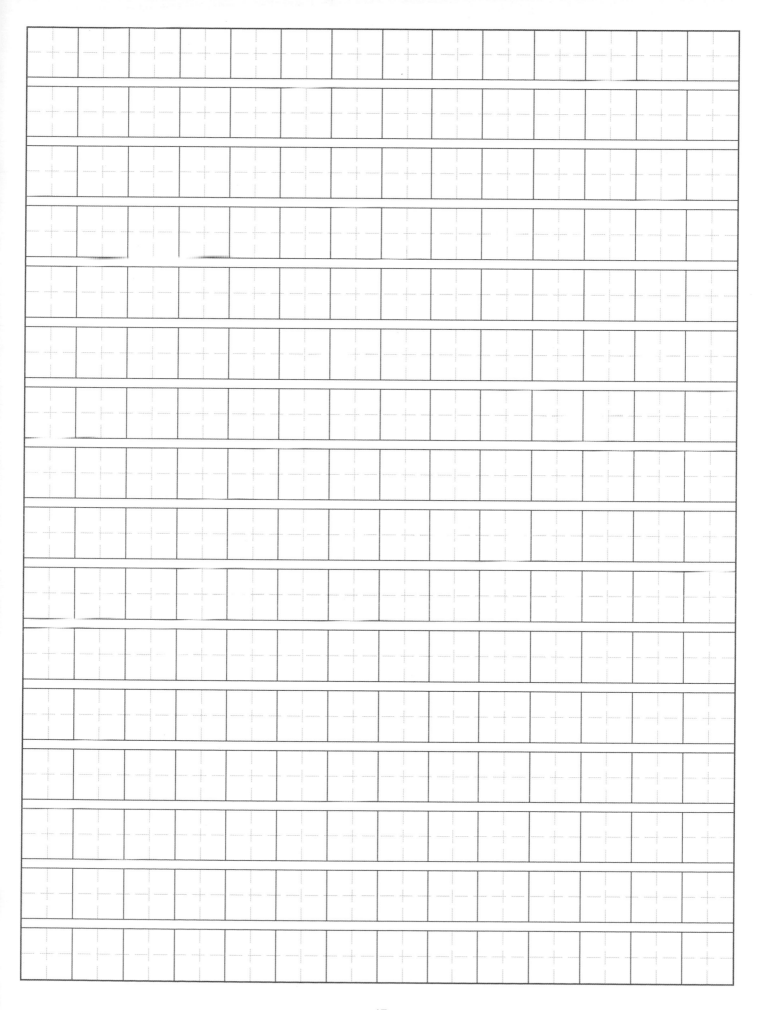

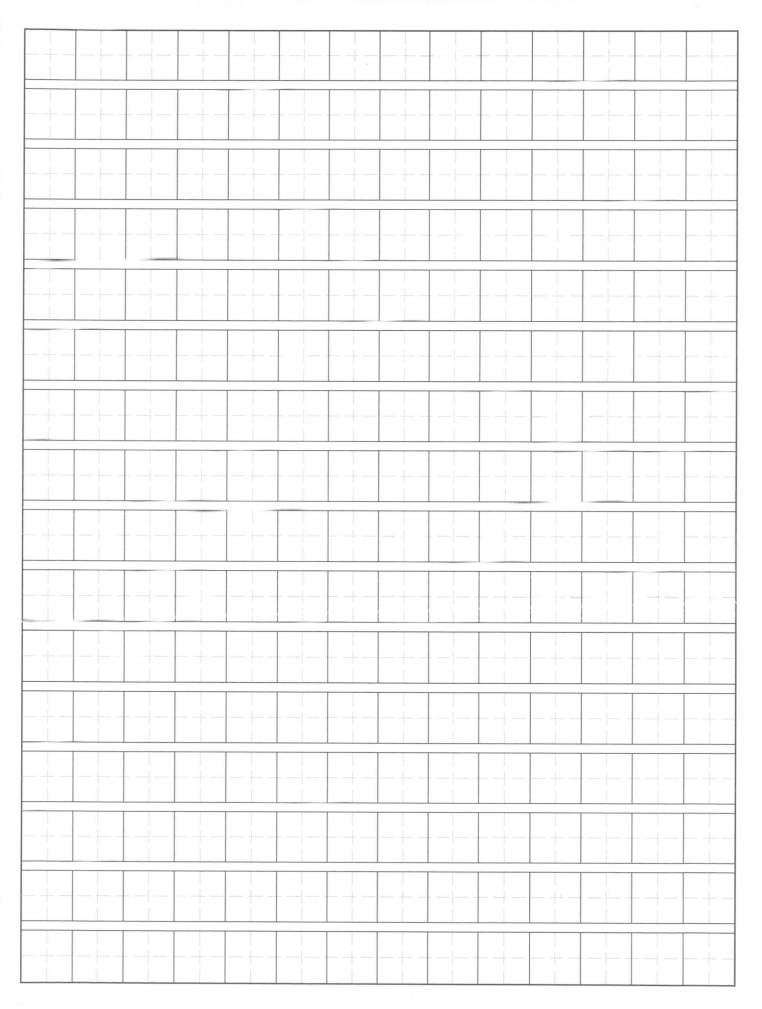

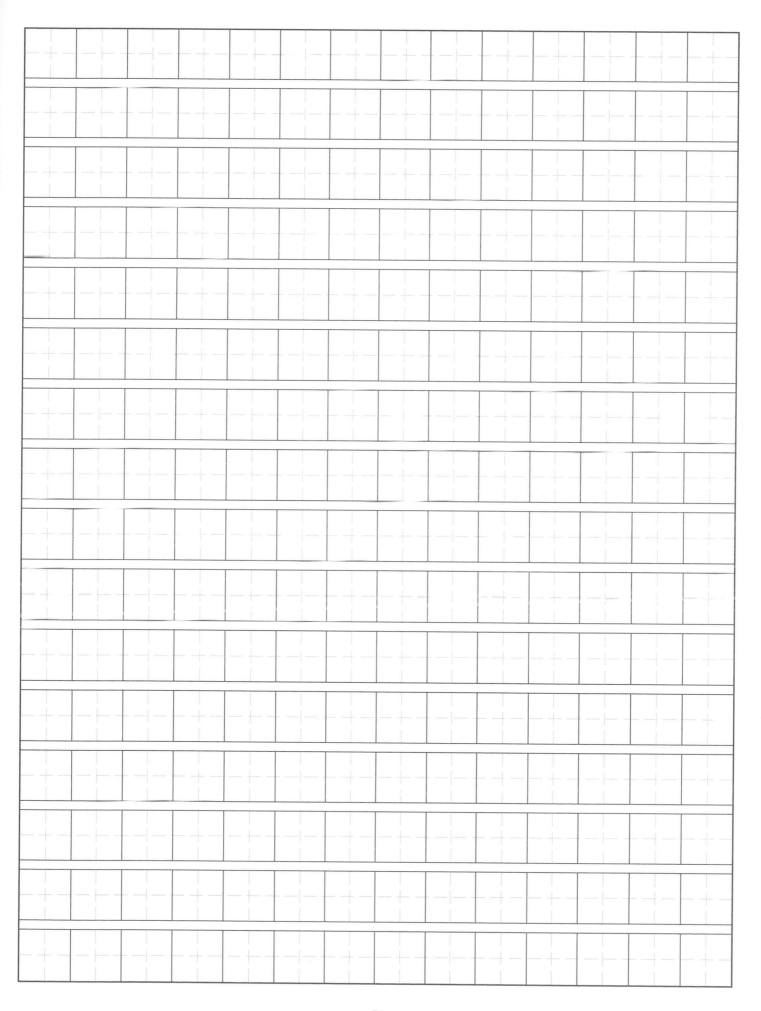

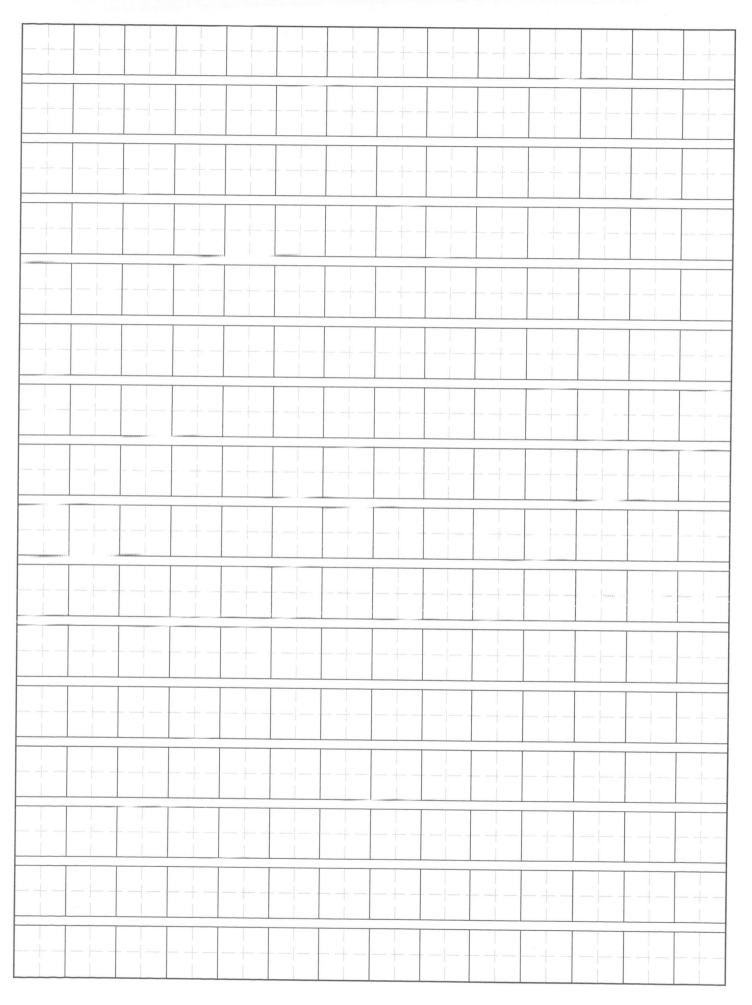

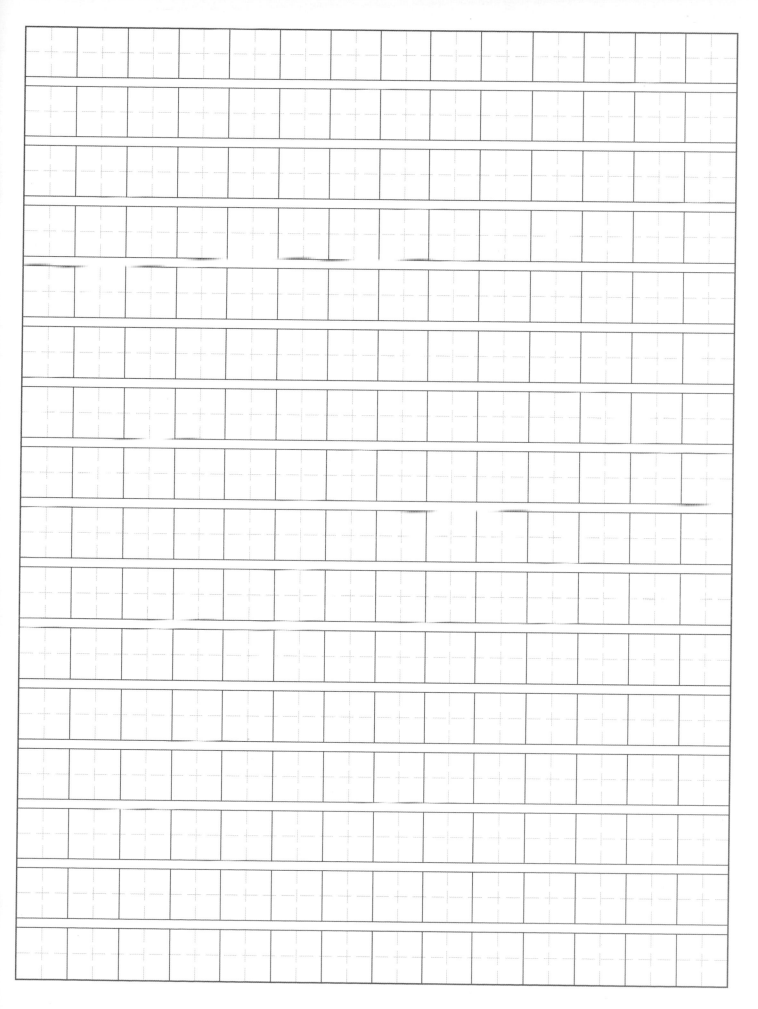

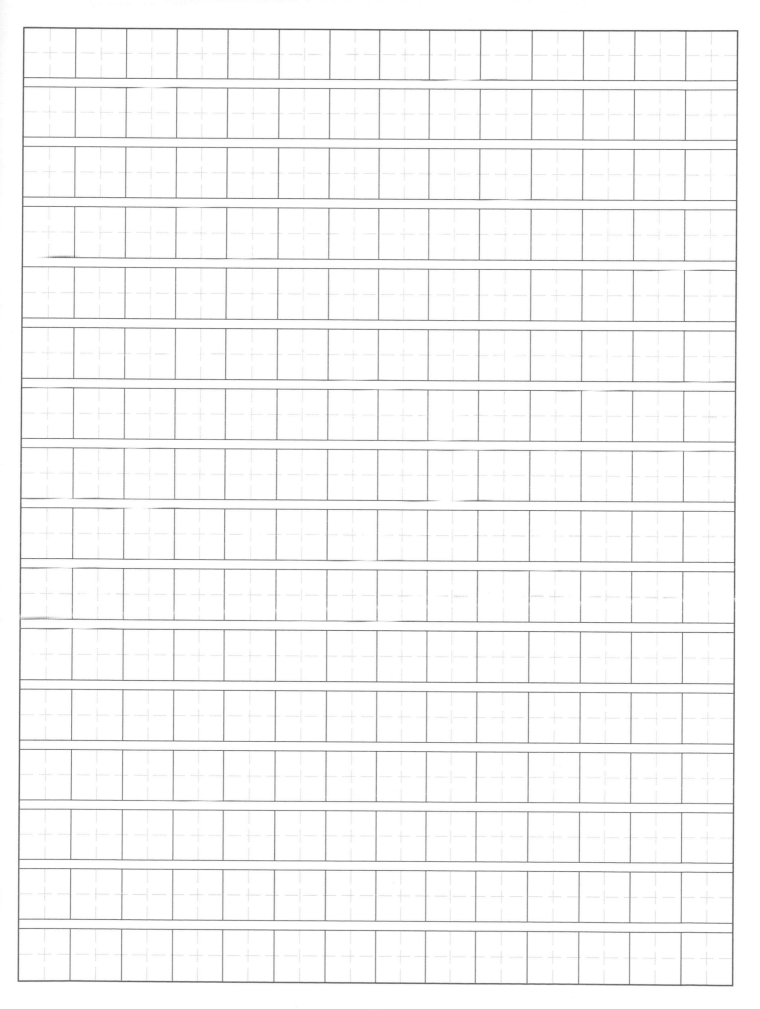

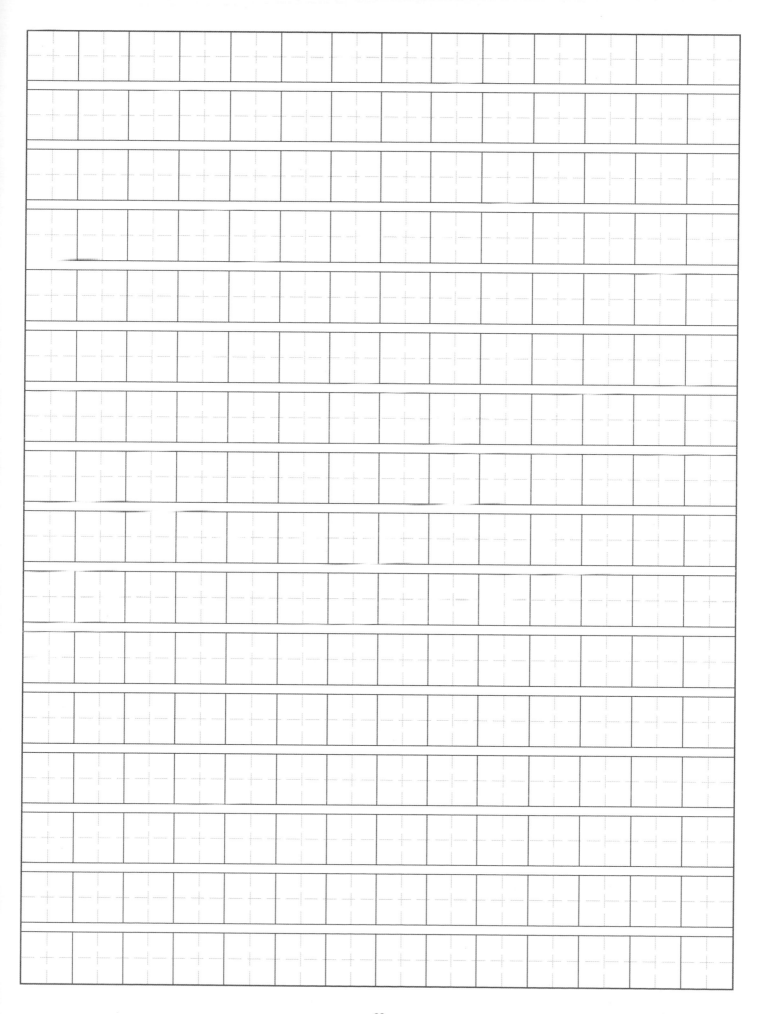

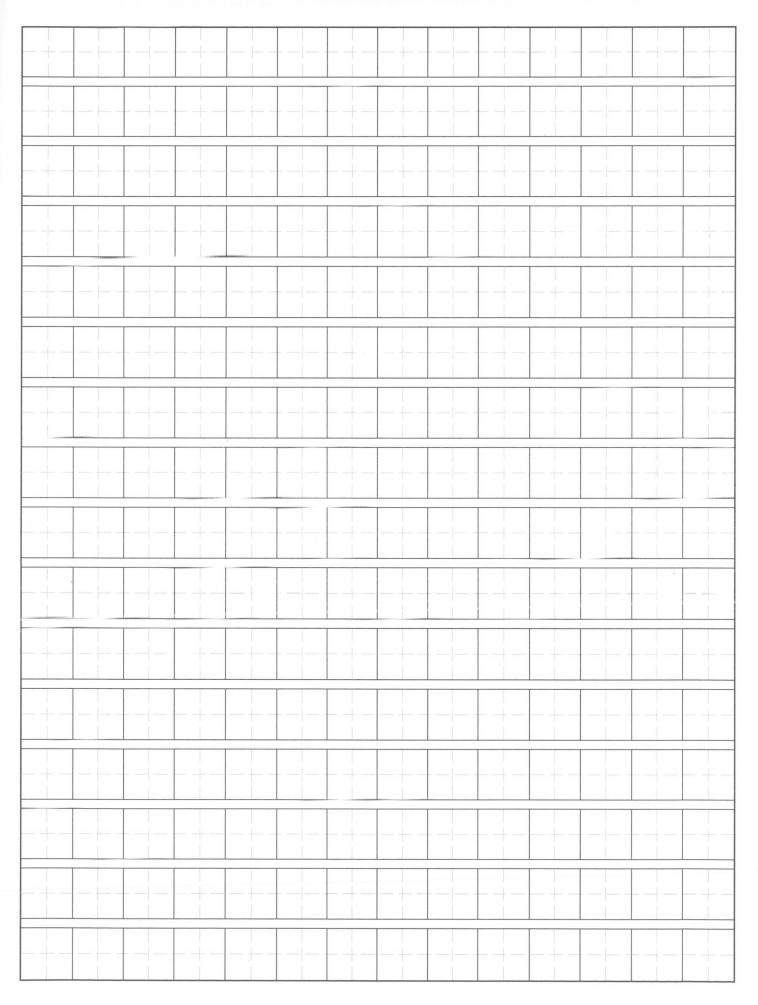

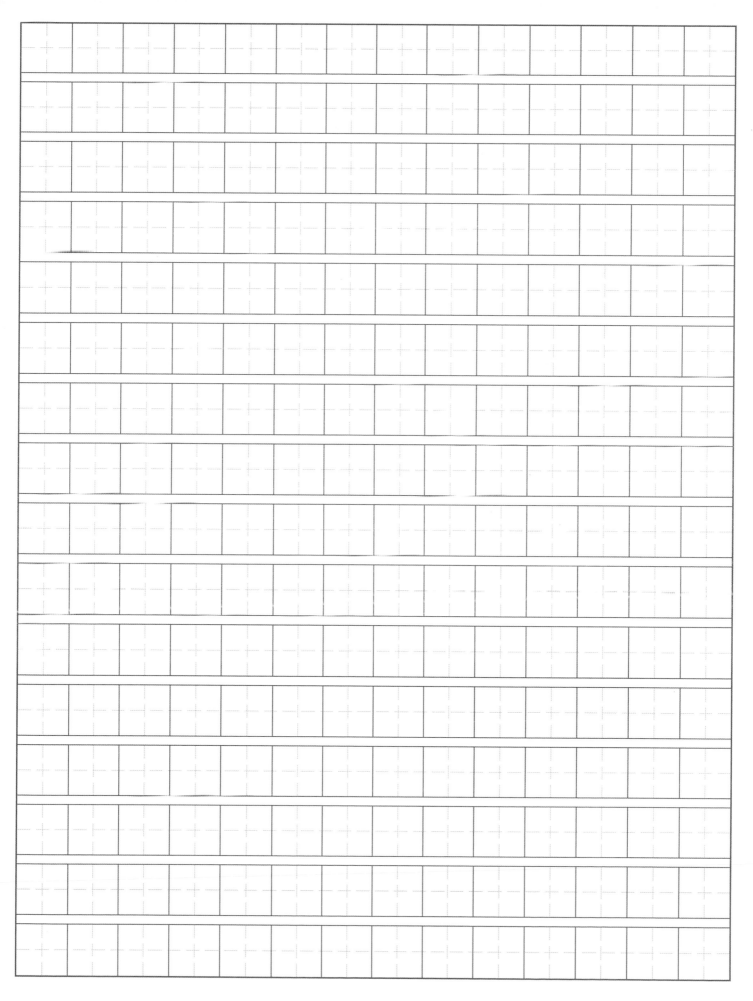

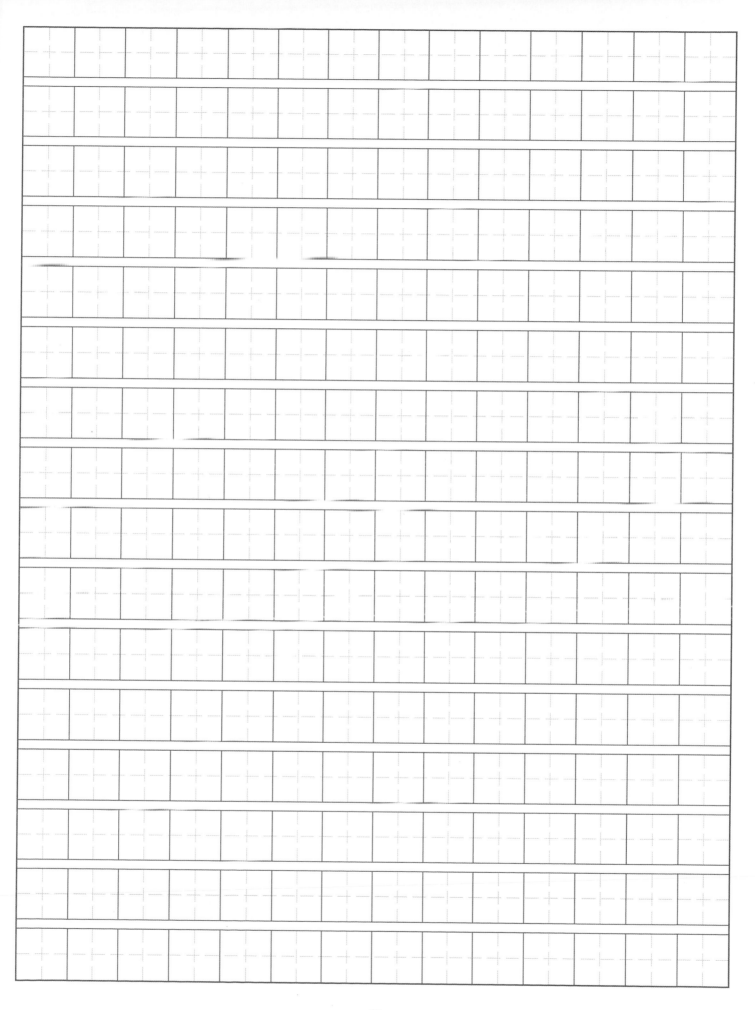

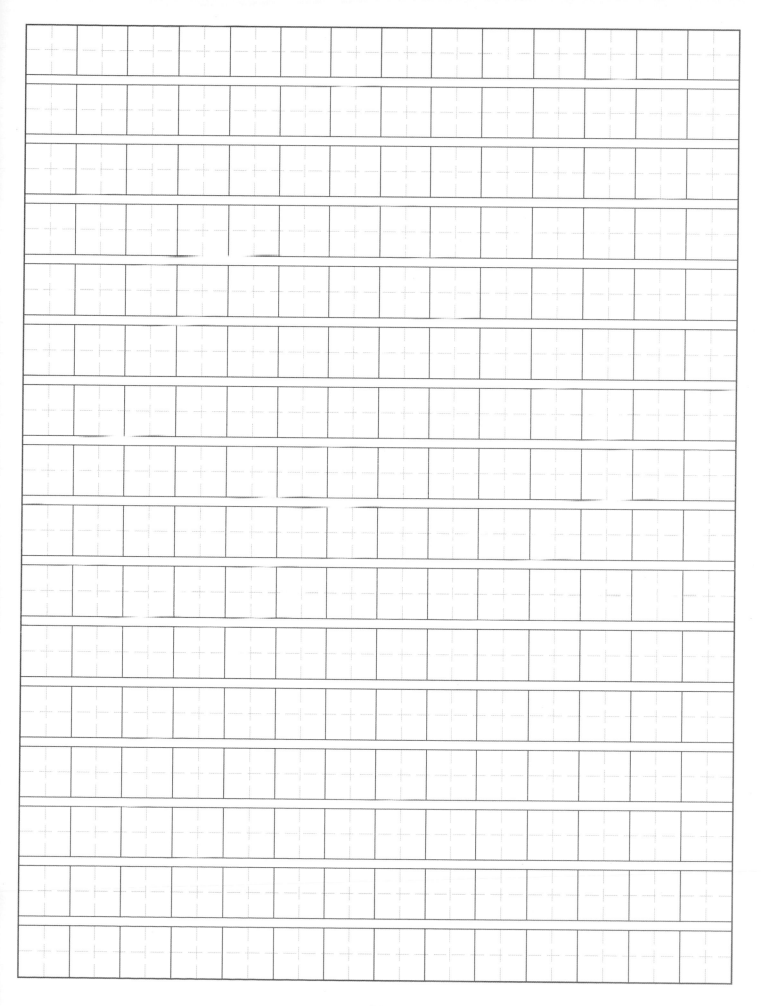

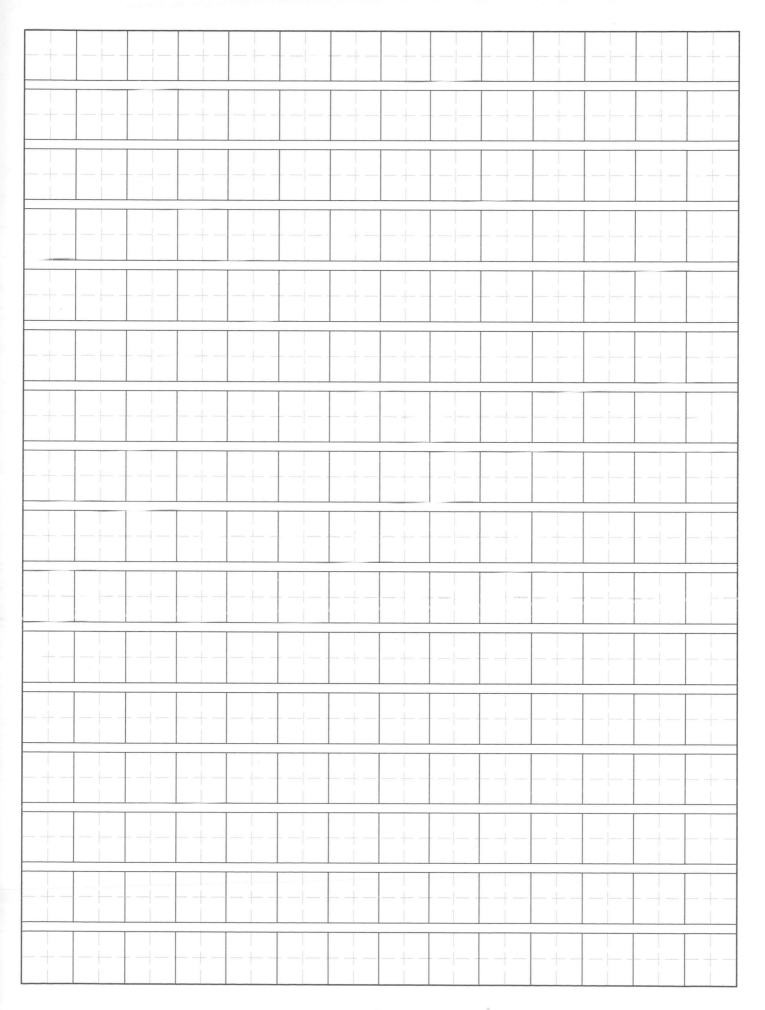

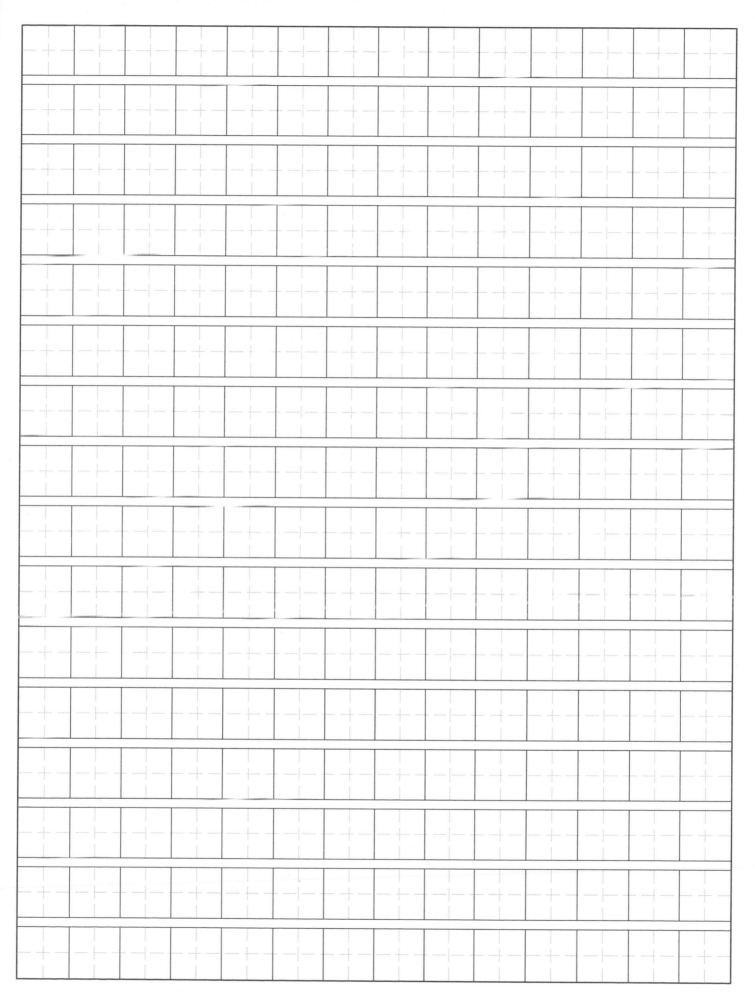

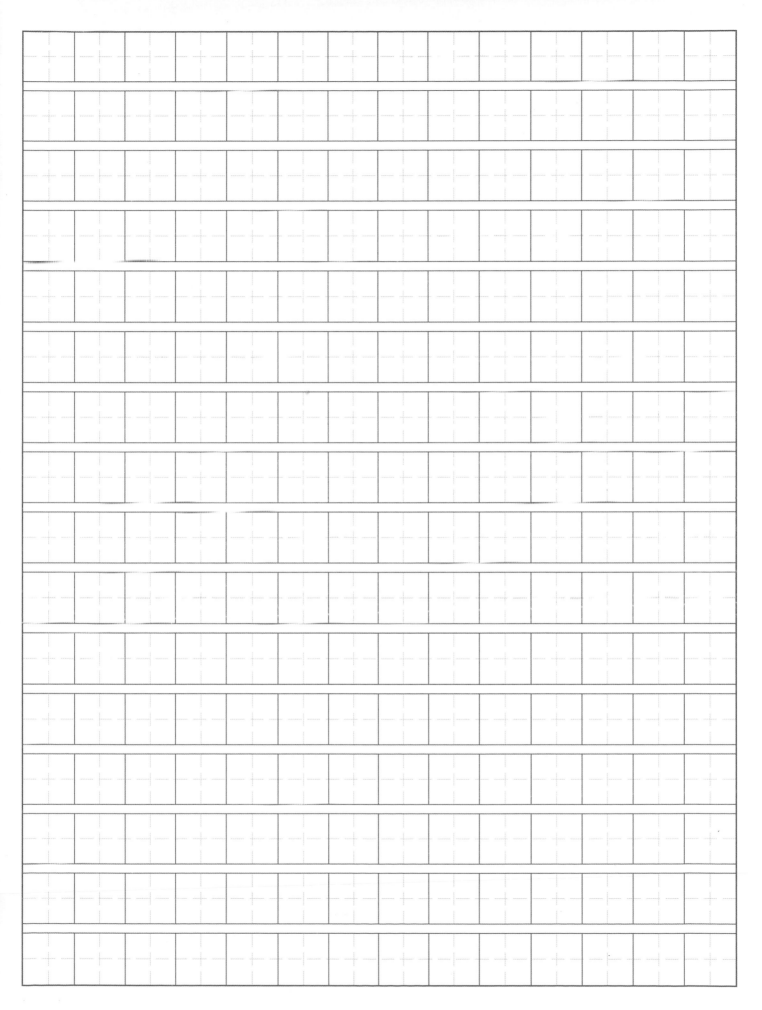

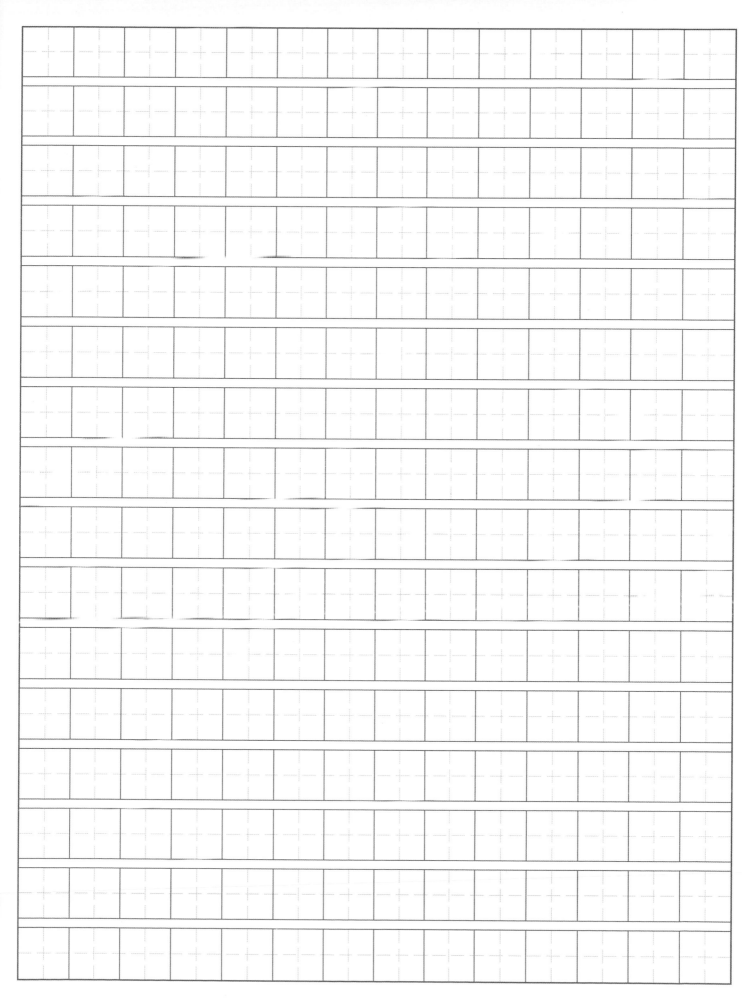

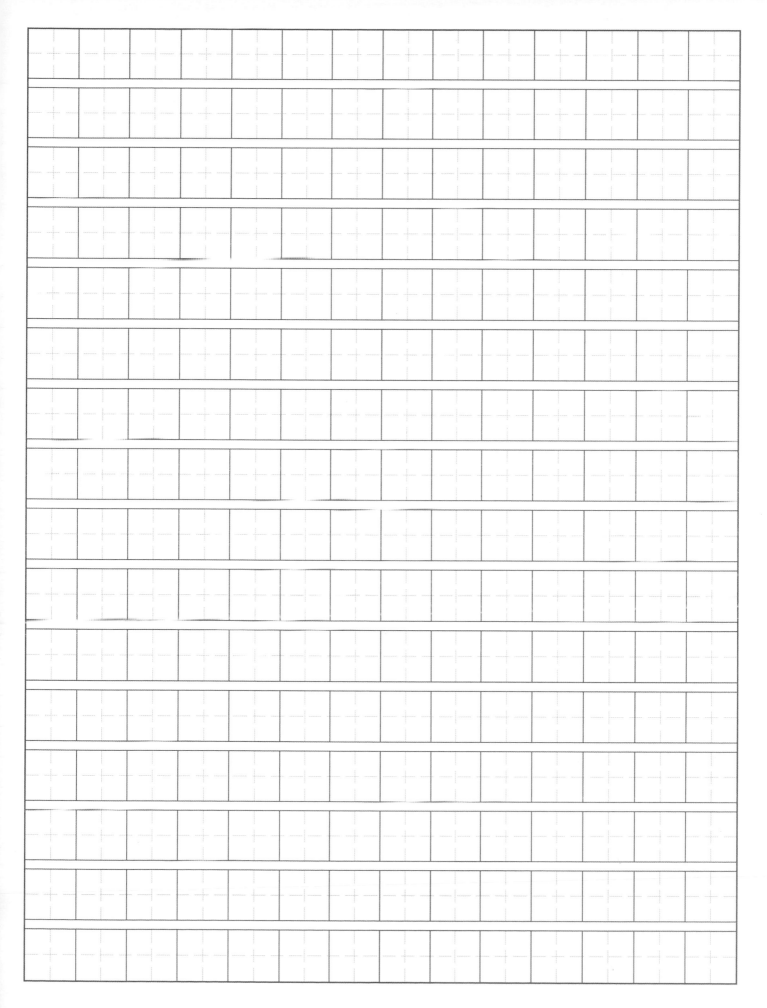

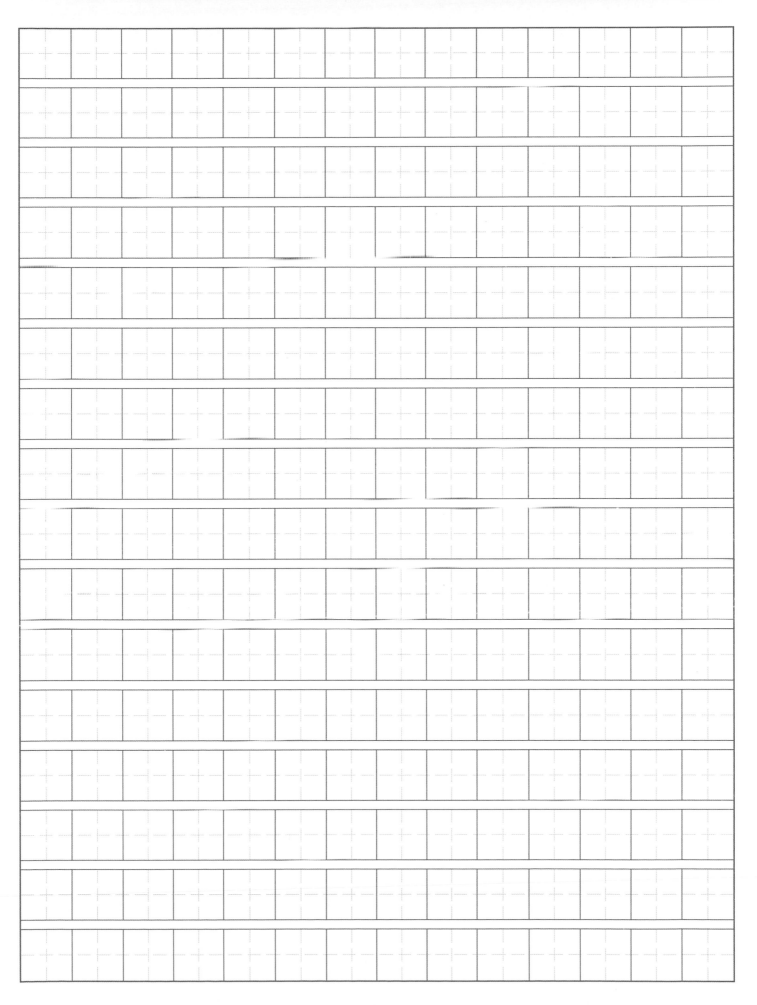

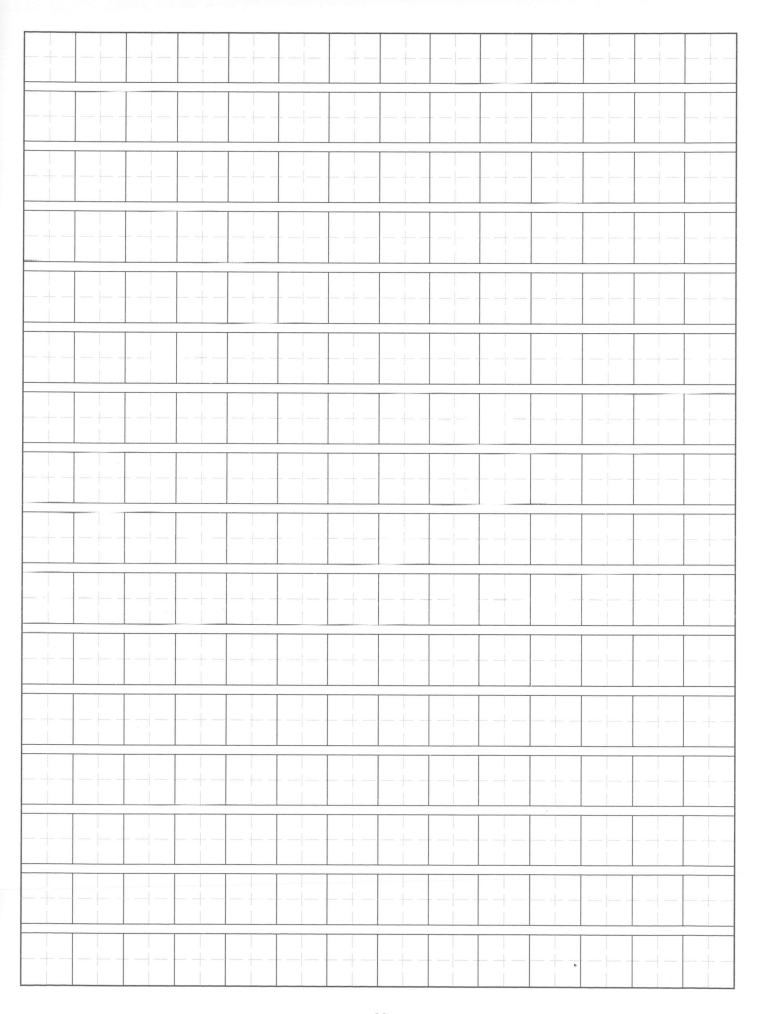

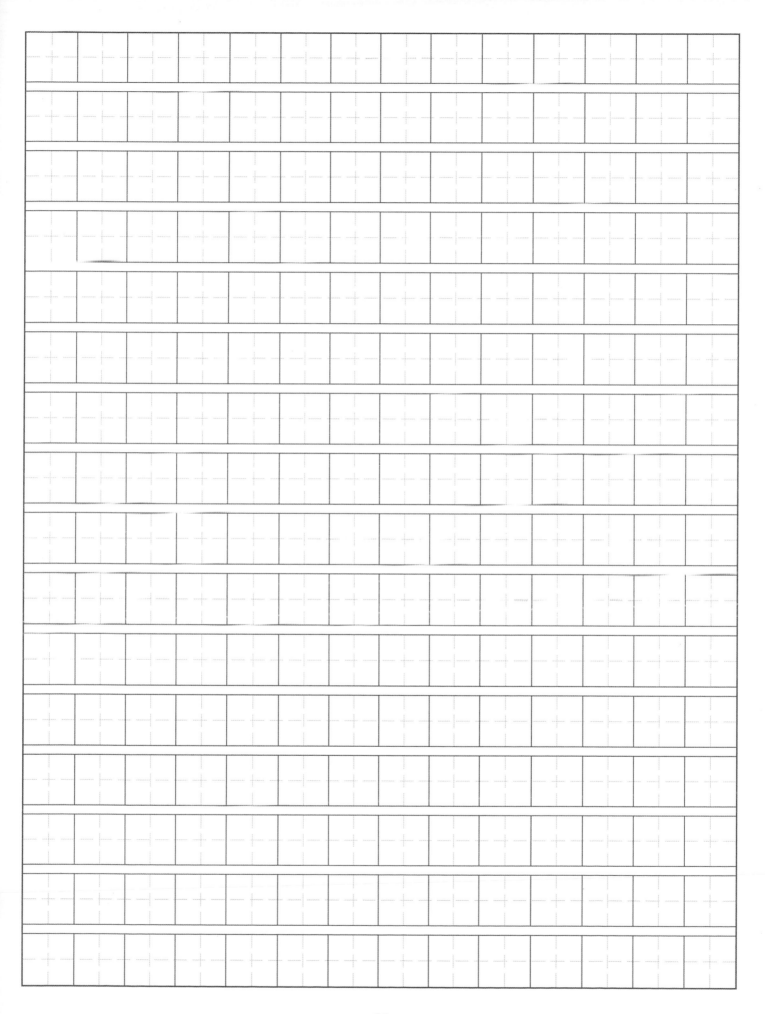

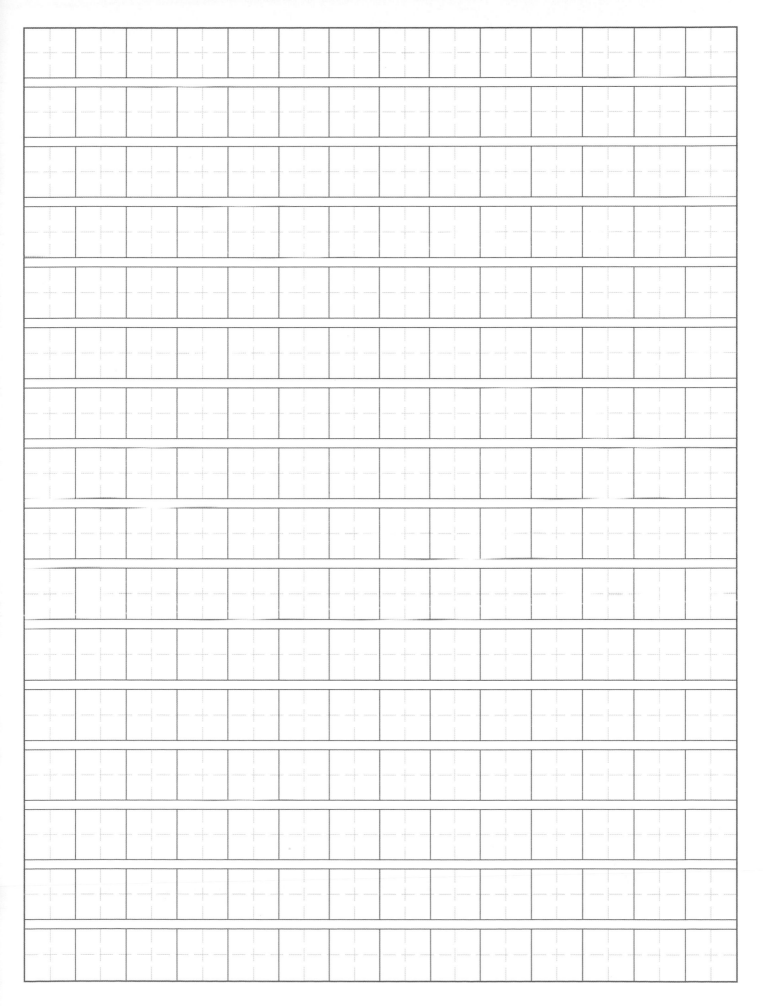

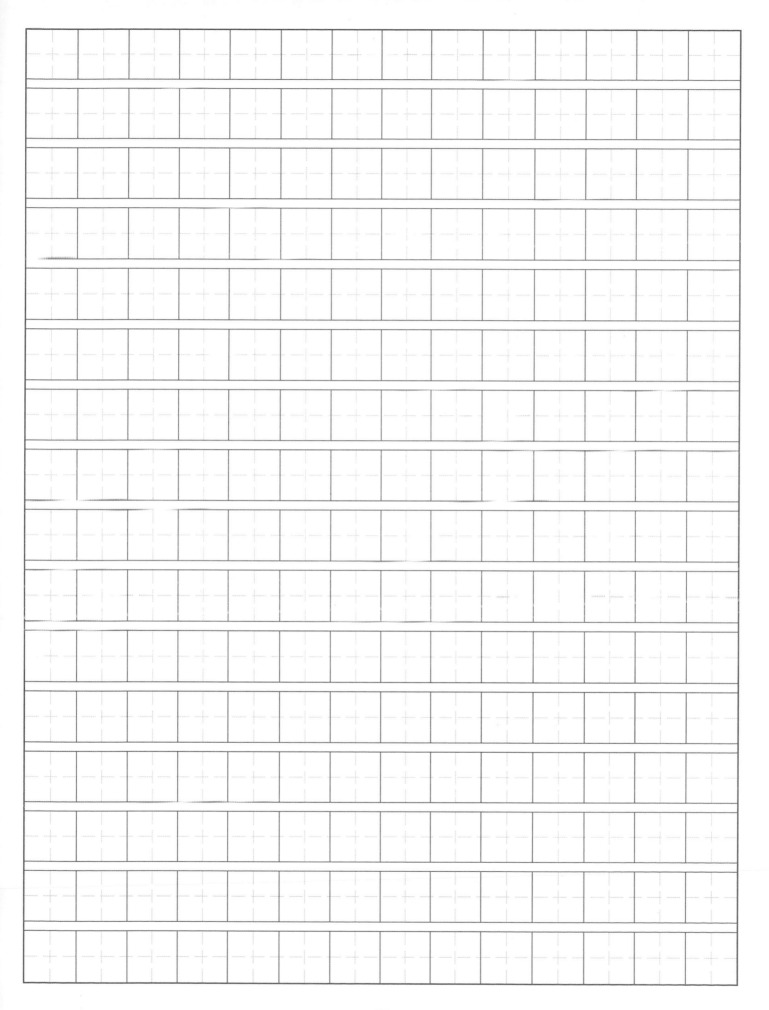

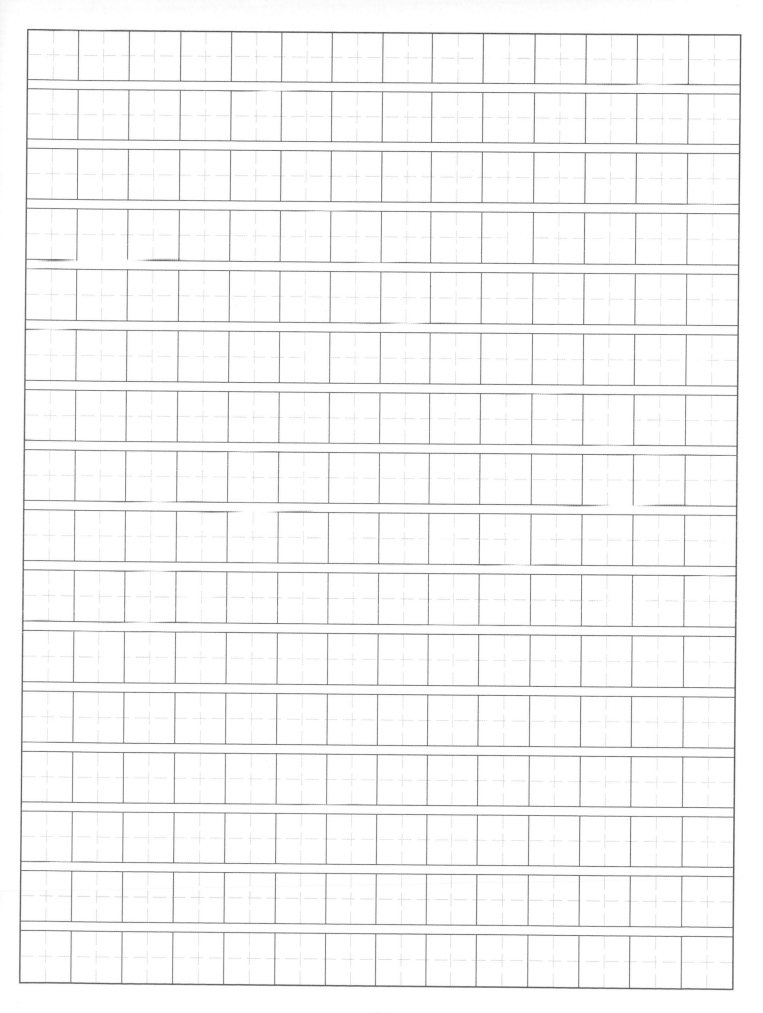

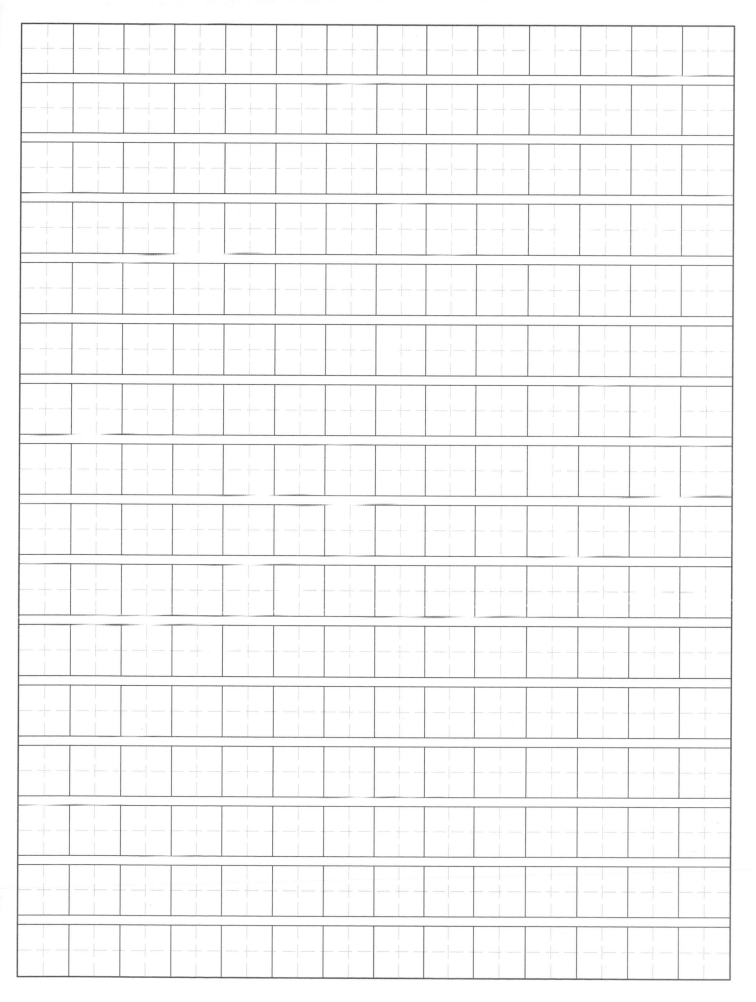

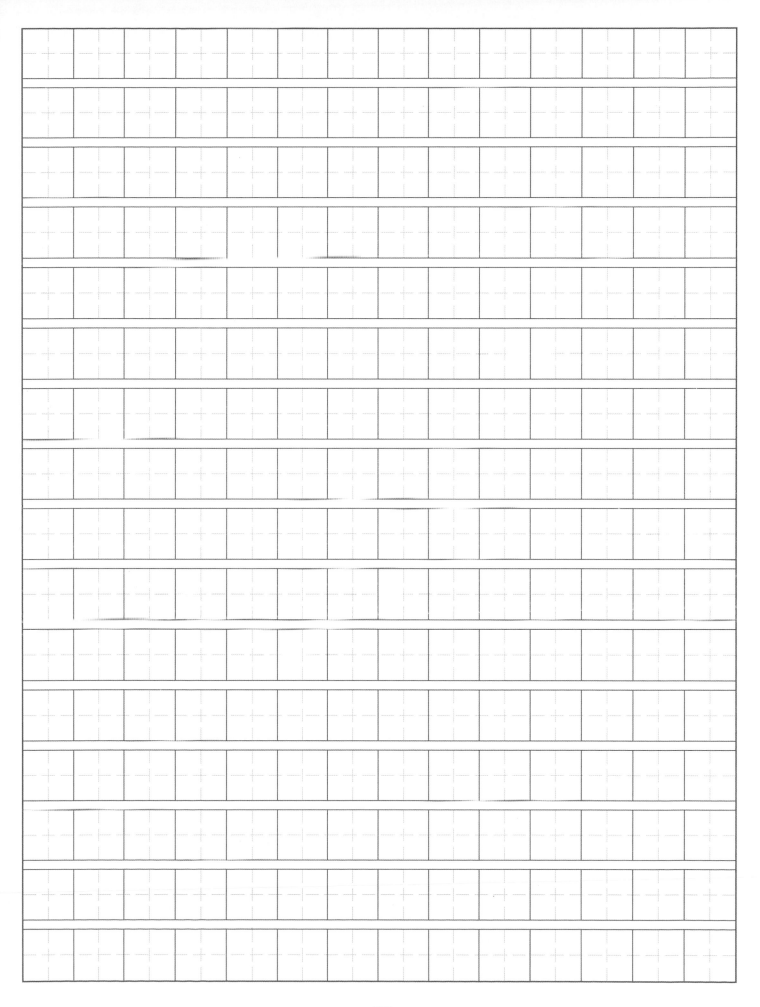

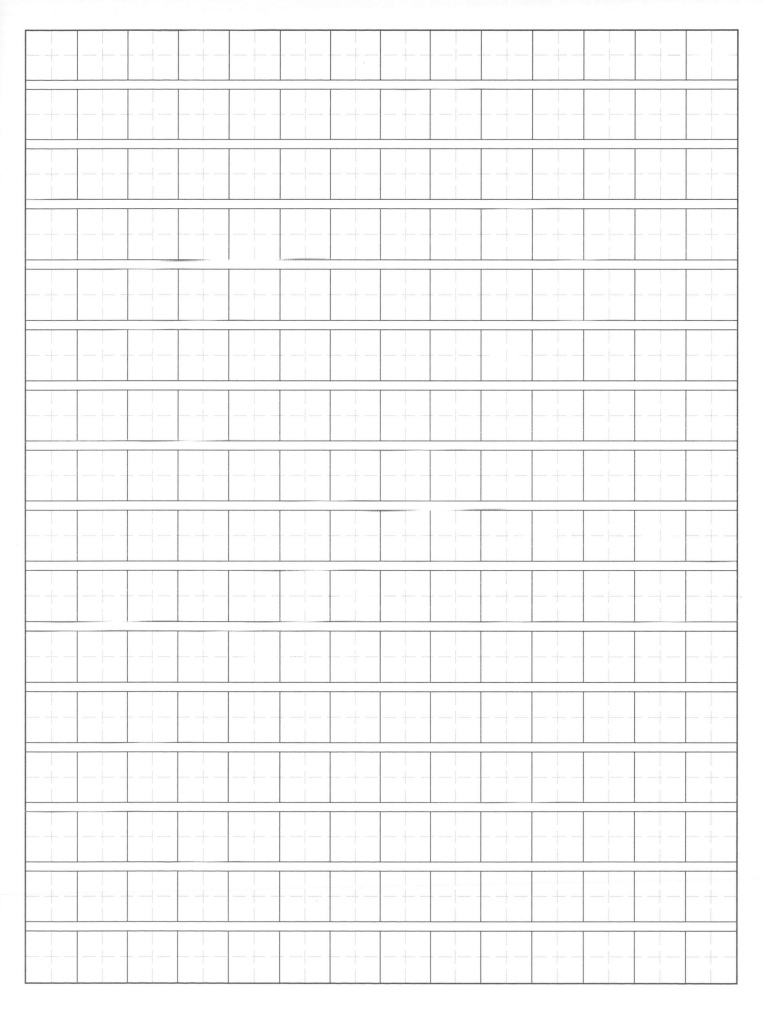

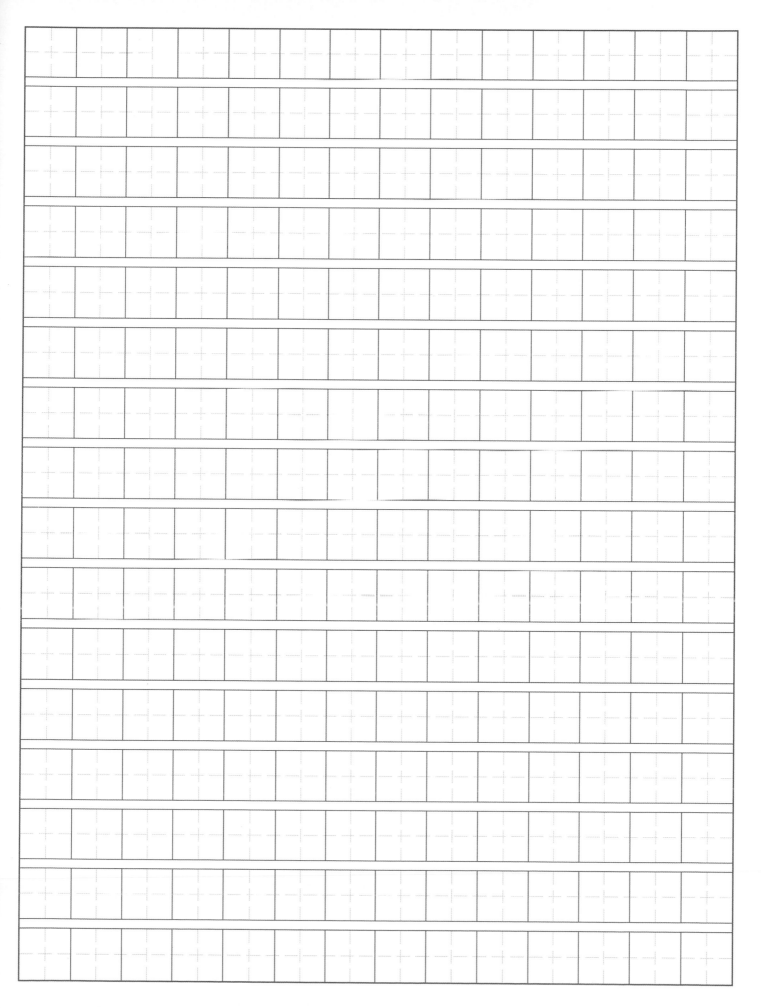

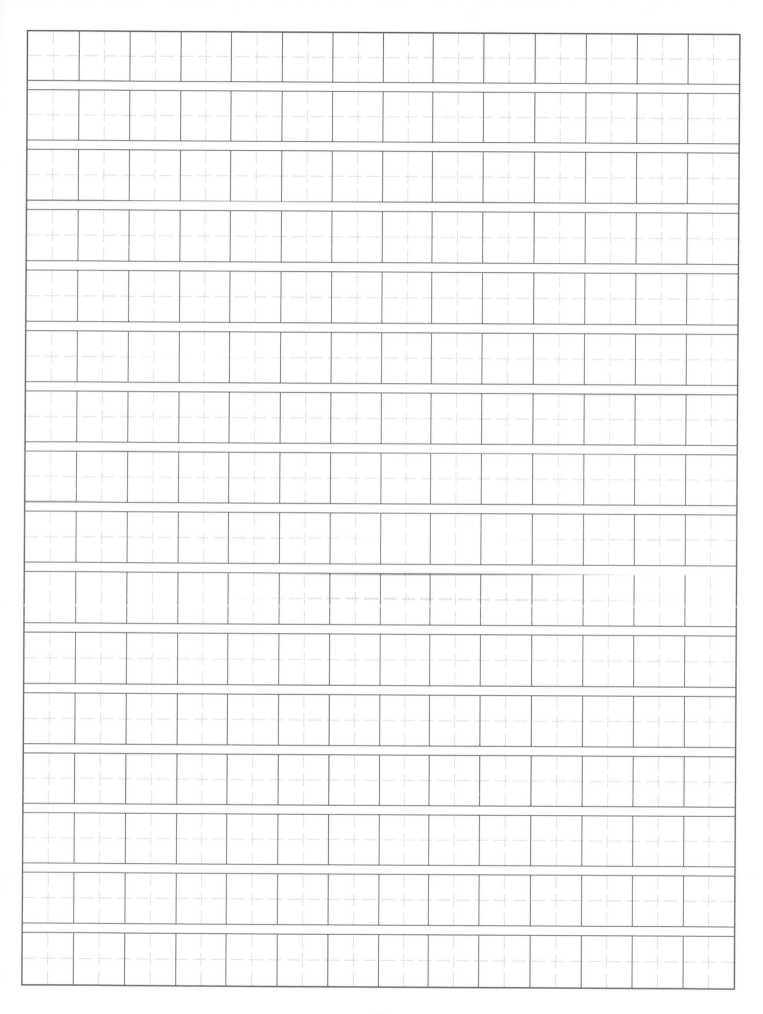

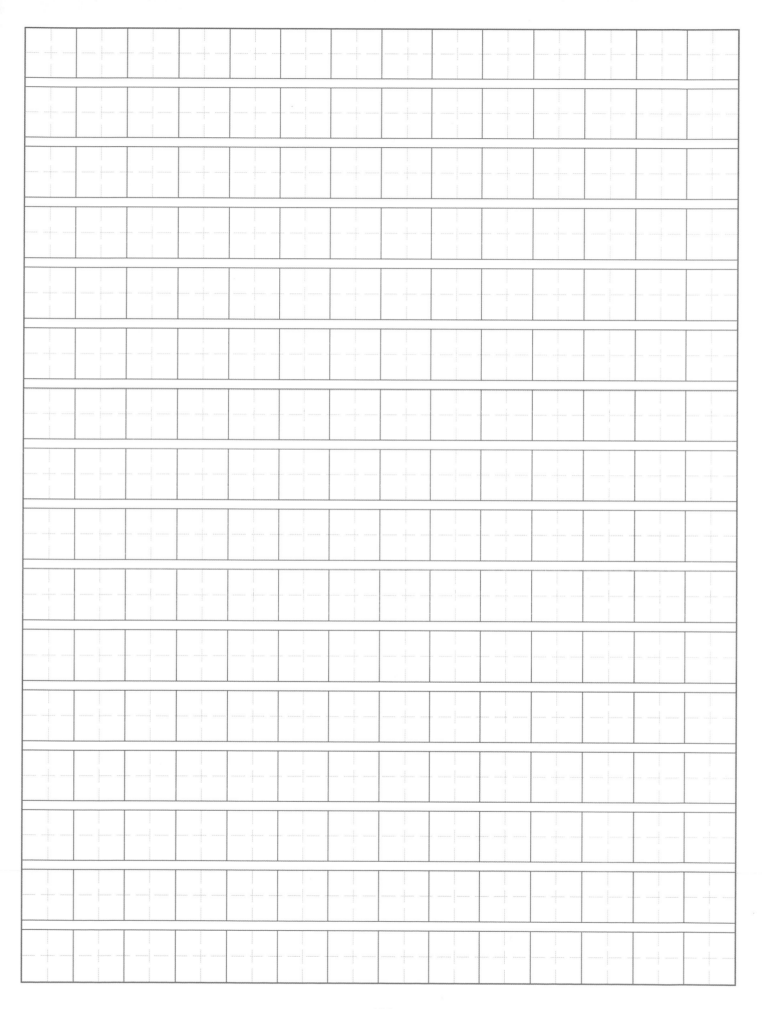

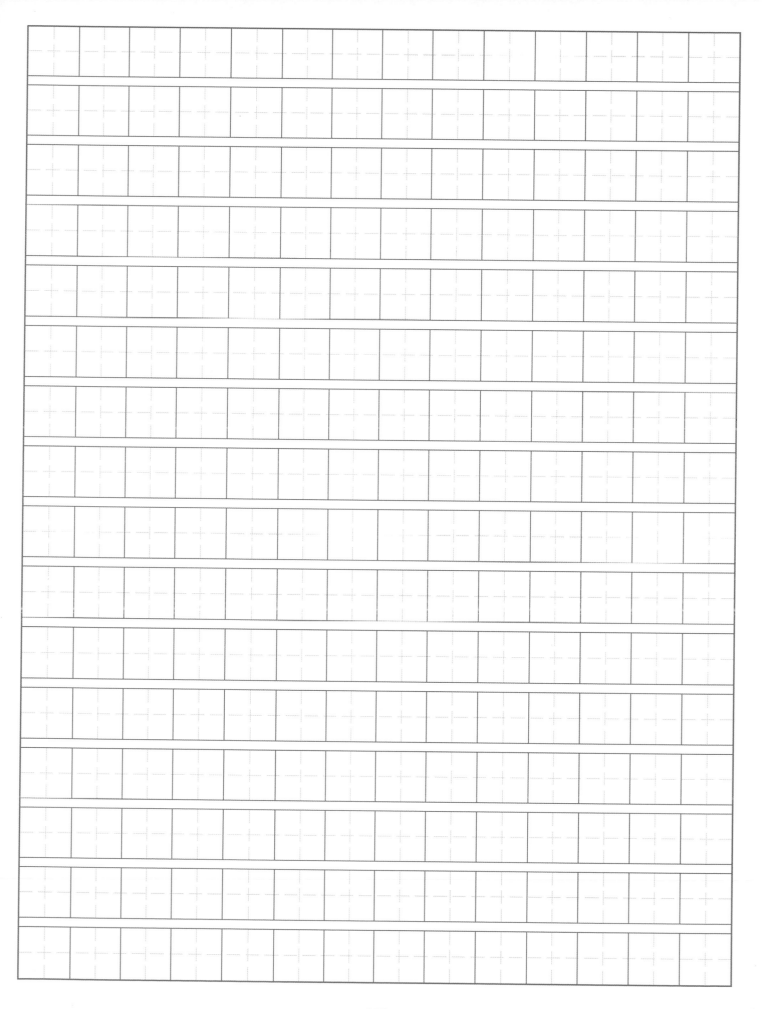

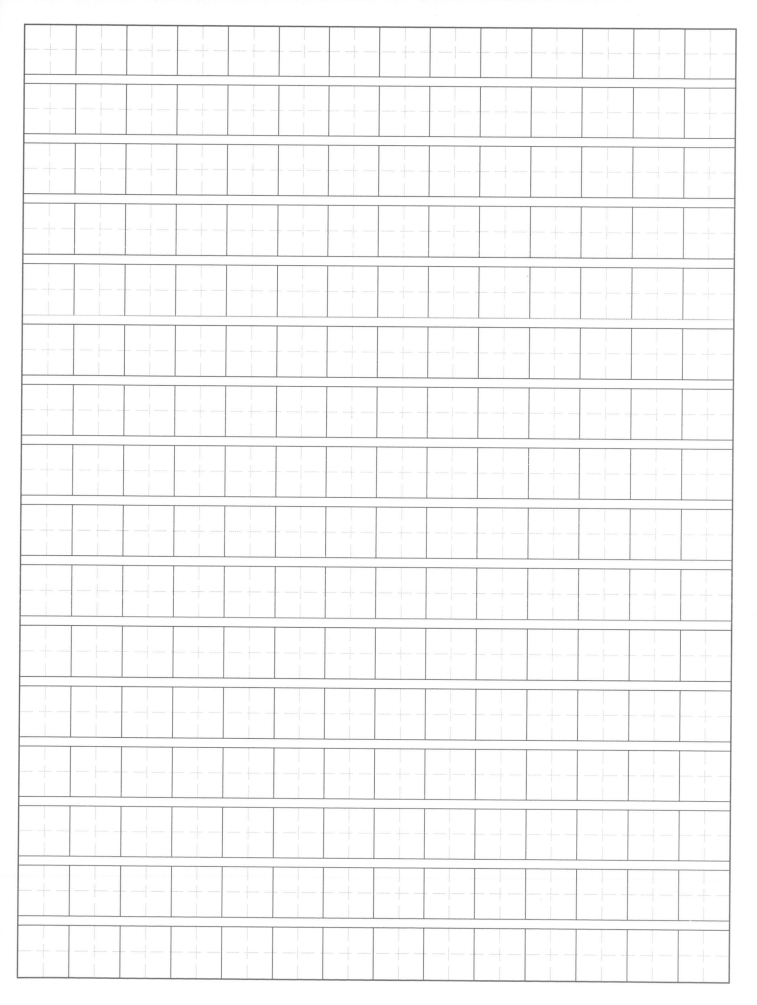

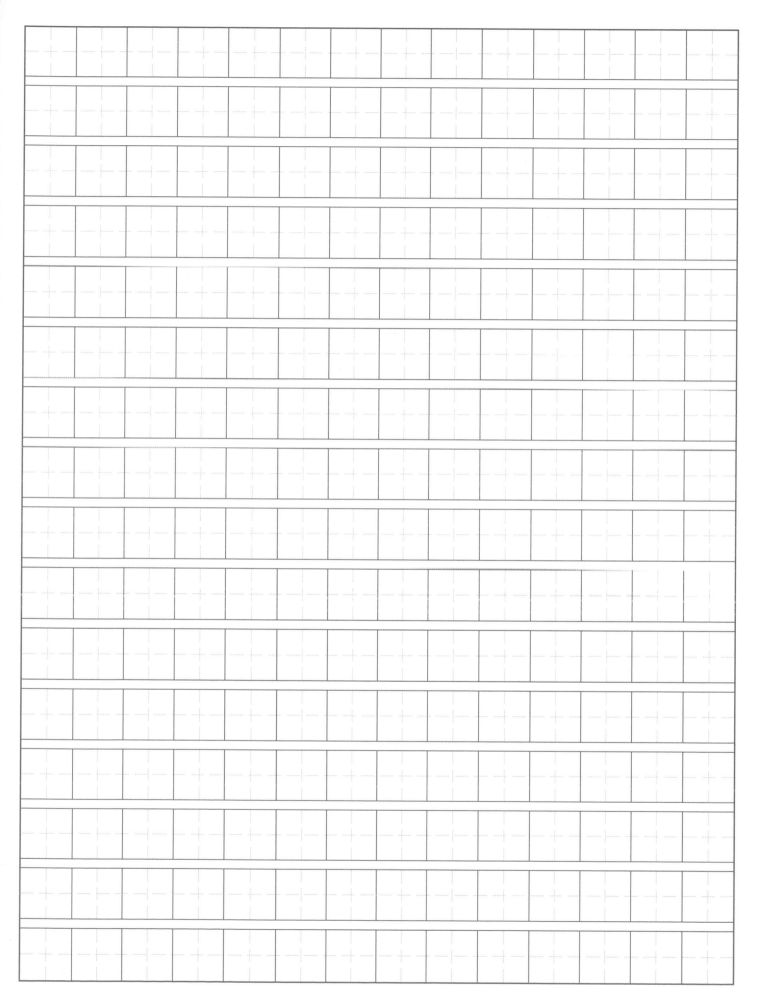

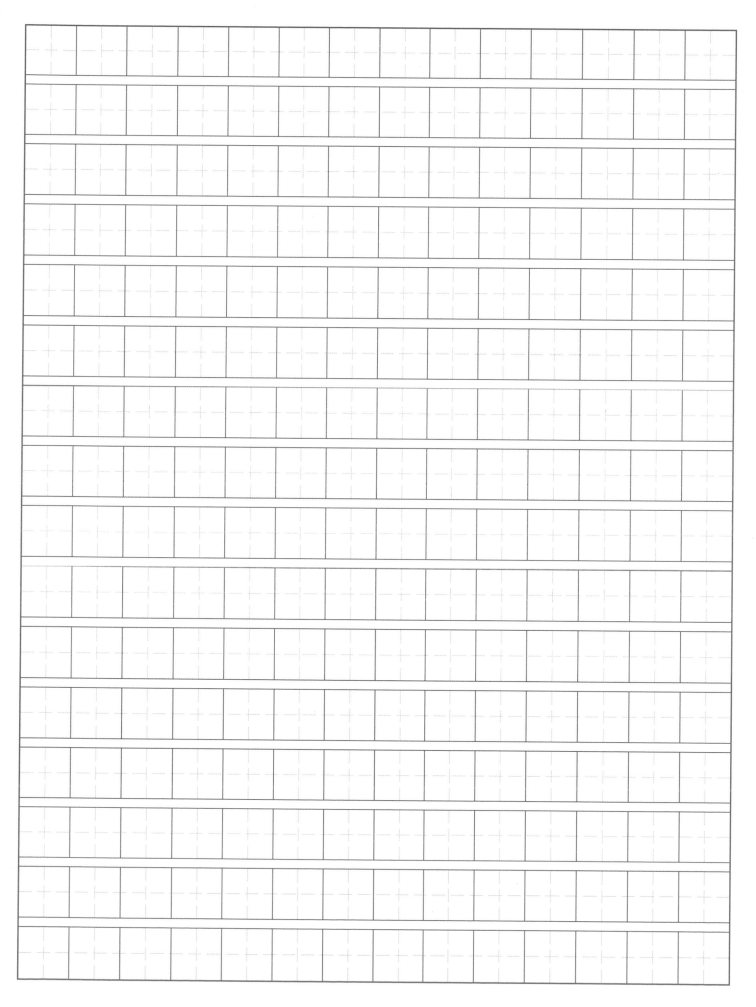

"Books to Span the East and West"

Tuttle Publishing was founded in 1832 in the small New England town of Rutland, Vermont [USA]. Our core values remain as strong today as they were then—to publish best-in-class books which bring people together one page at a time. In 1948, we established a publishing office in Japan—and Tuttle is now a leader in publishing English-language books about the arts, languages and cultures of Asia. The world has become a much smaller place today and Asia's economic and cultural influence has grown. Yet the need for meaningful dialogue and information about this diverse region has never been greater. Over the past seven decades, Tuttle has published thousands of books on subjects ranging from martial arts and paper crafts to language learning and literature—and our talented authors, illustrators, designers and photographers have won many prestigious awards. We welcome you to explore the wealth of information available on Asia at www.tuttlepublishing.com. at **www.tuttlepublishing.com**.

Published by Tuttle Publishing, an imprint of
Periplus Editions (HK) Ltd.

www.tuttlepublishing.com

Copyright © 2022 by Periplus Editions (HK) Ltd.
Pages 1 and 3 by Tina Cho.
Pages 12–19 by Yeon-Jeong Kim.

ISBN 978-0-8048-5560-0

Distributed by

North America, Latin America & Europe
Tuttle Publishing
364 Innovation Drive
North Clarendon,
VT 05759-9436 U.S.A.
Tel: 1 (802) 773-8930; Fax: 1 (802) 773-6993
info@tuttlepublishing.com; www.tuttlepublishing.com

Asia Pacific
Berkeley Books Pte. Ltd.
3 Kallang Sector #04-01
Singapore 349278
Tel: (65) 6741 2178; Fax: (65) 6741 2179
inquiries@periplus.com.sg; www.tuttlepublishing.com

25 25 24 23 22
10 9 8 7 6 5 4 3 2 1

Printed in Singapore   2207TP